# The
# Changing
# Face
# of British
# Retailing

© Newman Books Ltd
First published September 1987
by Newman Books Ltd
48 Poland Street
London W1V 4PP
Tel: 01-439 3321

Printed in Great Britain by
Chandlers (Printers) Ltd, Bexhill-on-Sea, East Sussex


ISBN 0 7079 6942 5

# Contents

Foreword   v
*Richard Weir*

Introduction   vii
*Edward McFadyen*

The fashion revolution   1
*Penelope Ody*

The strategic significance of design   14
*Rodney Fitch & James Woudhuysen*

EPoS and the retailer's information needs   22
*Dr Gil Jones*

The credit explosion   33
*Steve Worthington*

EFTPoS and non-cash payment systems   42
*Eric Foster & Martin Houghton*

Trends in food retailing   52
*Dr John Beaumont*

Out of town exodus   64
*Dr Russell Schiller*

Shop location analysis   74
*Dr David Rogers*

Trends in Physical Distribution   84
*Tony Rudd*

Convenience stores   94
*Dr David Kirby*

The Changing Consumer   103
*Michael Poynor*

Developments in education and training   114
*Montague Lewis*

Mergers and acquisitions   126
*Roger Cox*

About the authors   135

# Foreword

## by Richard Weir
### *Director-General, The Retail Consortium*

One only needs to glance at the headlines in the daily newspapers to appreciate the significance of the changes taking place in the high street. Some of these changes affect the structure of retailing, and involve the formation of larger and more diverse groups, crossing many of the traditional boundaries which used to divide one kind of retail business from another. The largest retailers are now among the leading companies in the UK in terms of size, while in terms of profitability, they can hold their own with any industrial sector.

However, not all the changes we learn about in the newspapers concern corporate finance, mergers and takeovers. New developments are emerging in the presentation of merchandise, in the method of store operation, the use of technology and, indeed, in the basic format of shops. New kinds of retailing are appearing, often operated on the franchise pattern, where a niche in the marketplace has been identified, and a previously unsuspected consumer need satisfied. Large retail developments in the centre, or on the edge, of towns, as well as green field sites, have dramatically changed the shopping environment familiar to customers.

These new developments constitute an alternative to the traditional high street — offering ample car parking and the space in which to create an entertaining as well as functional atmosphere. The high street fights back with a, perhaps, more sophisticated blend of recreational and leisure activities to complement the pull of its well-established shopping facilities. Even for those of us for whom retailing is our working life, there is a need for a guidebook to alert us to significant changes, and to distinguish enduring trends from mere flashes in the pan.

I therefore heartily welcome the publication of a book which is both informative and authoritative. Each of the contributors is an acknowledged expert in the field, and is eminently qualified to guide us through the labyrinth of change.

The emergence of the retail sector as an important contributor to the creation of wealth and the enhancement of people's lives is now well established. This book underscores both the achievements to date and the potential for the future. I strongly recommend it to the reader.

# Introduction

## Edward McFadyen
*Editor, Retail & Distribution Management*


This book is by way of being a celebration. Over the past few years it has become clear that the UK retail sector is a success story. For too long successive British governments have treated the retail sector as of secondary importance ("they don't actually *produce* anything, you understand old boy"); for years British retailers have suffered discrimination from government policies that favour manufacturing industry. And for too long British retailers have accepted, with tired resignation, European comments that if you want to see good professional retailing of a high standard, you should go to America, or France, or wherever, but certainly don't bother to have a look round the UK.

This is no longer true. British retailers now have quite a lot that they can be pleased about; for most of the larger companies, good financial performances sustained over a long period; throughout the sector as a whole, a stream of innovative techniques; the refurbishment and regeneration of leading retailers; in sum, a story of imagination and flair.

This book sets out to chart the main points of this story, to put solid achievement firmly on record. It is not slavishly sycophantic; most of our contributors, while outlining the considerable changes that have taken place, have seized the opportunity to be properly critical of things that are yet left undone, of improvements that might yet be made.

A crucial date for British retailing was spring 1982, when Hepworth re-launched the Kendall chain as Next. In her chapter on the fashion revolution, Penelope Ody points out that "almost overnight, Next appeared to transform shopping patterns. It also became an instant cult. Outlets were forced to close as the crush of customers built up or ran out of stock, and Next clones began to proliferate as other retailers sniffed success and leapt unashamedly onto the bandwaggon".

This was the beginning of niche marketing — identifying and brilliantly exploiting a segment of the market that was uncatered for — in this case the 25-45-year-old aspiring career woman. It ran parallel, in the early 1980s, with a decline in the youth market, partly because of youth unemployment and partly because of a drop in teenage population.

The 1980s also saw the successful revitalisation of that old retail warhorse, the Burton Group. With its takeover of Debenhams, it began to exercise segmented merchandising at a multi-strategy level, as Roger Cox describes it, where a retailer operates from several different chains of shops each closely targeted to a specific market.

Stores also took to lifestyle merchandising in the 1980s. Debenhams and the House of Fraser led the way, and the repercussions began to make themselves felt the length of the High Street. The variety chains, with what seems like growing insecurity, launched major refurbishment programmes — Littlewoods, British Home Stores, even Marks & Spencer. As Roger Cox says, British Home Stores became BhS because it was being left behind by more aggressive multiple retailers selling similar ranges with more flair and marketing skill.

Marks & Spencer tried to remain faithful to St Michael, Penelope Ody reminds us, but found during 1983-84 that its women's clothing sales were slipping for perhaps the first time in its history. It responded by completely revamping its presentation and merchandise mix. Out went gondolas and in came hanging rail presentation and clothes geared to a more fashion conscious shopper. "M&S", she writes, "has clearly seen which way the fashion wind was blowing in the High Street and has trimmed its sales accordingly".

And what has been happening in the food sector? John Beaumont of the Institute of Grocery Distribution charts the inexorable growth of the superstore, both in numbers and in sheer size. "There has been", he writes,"a significant move into superstores having a sales area in excess of 25,000 sq ft". Within these massive units, with an average sales area of some 38,000 sq ft, the trend towards diversification into non-food which characterised the 1970s has now given way to an emphasis on food, and particularly fresh foods. Substantial space given over to fresh produce and to in-store bakeries is now a commonplace, as is the increasing attention being given by the major multiples to health foods — no longer a minority fad.

Price, the major marketing weapon of the grocery multiples in the 1970s, has now been replaced by quality. As John Beaumont writes, "the increasing emphasis on quality and the need to differentiate particular retailing images has permeated the entire business operation of most major grocers". This has emphasised their determination to take on a central role in marketing; central to this has been the growth of retailers' own brands.

While most large mixed retailers have tended to drop food from their ranges — notably Woolworth and British Home Stores — the redoubtable Marks & Spencer confounded the critics by making a spectacular success out of its food operation, which now has sales approaching £1,500m.

In fact there's no doubt that the major grocery retailers are returning to selling what they're best at — food. The announcement in May 1987 that Presto and Safeway will not diversify into durables or fashion confirms this trend — and it makes sense in the current retail environment. When the big grocery groups such as Asda and Tesco moved into non-food, the clothing and DIY markets were theirs for the taking. But now we have a proliferation of specialist fashion groups, as we have already noted, and massive DIY stores such as Texas and B&Q.

## Fresh foods and quality

John Beaumont sees fresh foods and quality as the main competitive weapons of the 1980s (with price still remaining); for the 1990s he visualises the addition of range and service.

Underpinning all these changes in both the food and non-food sectors is one significant agent for change — design. No longer merely decorative, design has earned its place as an essential part of the merchandising policy, and a crucial aspect of niche marketing. Rodney Fitch and James Woudhuysen point out in their chapter that the consumer is now more conscious than ever of good design; young people, they say, have an instinctive sense of the mediocre.

With the enormous growth in the design business over the past five years or so has come a significant change in the designer's brief: an increasingly large number of specialist retailers, in areas as diverse as fashion, toys, records, or books, will see the role of the designer as crucial in formulating the message they wish to put over to that particular carefully defined "niche" which they have selected.

No perspective on the retail scene over the past few years would be complete without some appreciation of the function of technology. Since time began, writes Gil Jones, retailers have grappled with the essential problem of knowing precisely what they sell, and what they have in stock, at a fine enough level of detail to take meaningful operational decisions. The arrival of EPoS brought with it the possibility of solving this problem once and for all. And it is a problem which has become increasingly urgent over the past few years — not only because of the trend to segmented merchandising we have just commented on, and all that implies, but because of the highly intensified level of competition which is now endemic to the sector.

But retailers, says Gil Jones, "are not really interested in EPoS at all. They are only interested in solving the problems that EPoS is designed to solve". One result of this — and this is part of the second EPoS revolution which he argues is now taking place — is the emergence of "a plethora of software-led solutions . . . software packages that are designed to process the detailed data captured in the shop into meaningful and actionable reports".

Hence EPoS is beginning to be seen as just the starting-point in the retail information cycle, and a number of interesting new application areas are beginning to emerge. Space management is one; Direct Product Profitability (DPP), although not new, has reappeared on the scene with the realisation that it can be immensely more effective with the application of the personal computer. And although at present confined to the food sector, it can't be long before more sophisticated DPP models are constructed and the non-food sector begins to reap its advantages.

Traditional retailing in the UK currently has a turnover of some £90 billion, and retailers, according to Gil Jones, spend on average around 1 per cent of their gross turnover on information systems. The actual market penetration of EPoS in the UK retail sector is still quite low — around 10 per cent overall. Quite clearly, EPoS is big business.

Where does this £90 billion that people spend in the shops come from? Well of course the interesting thing is that they haven't actually got it — or all that much of it. Forget all that old stuff about our being a nation of shopkeepers — we are in fact a nation of borrowers. Credit is no longer discreditable; social attitudes have changed — now the more you owe the smarter you are. As Steve Worthington points out in his chapter on the Credit Explosion, retailers as well as banks have taken advantage of this, and companies like Marks & Spencer, Burton and the Storehouse group are becoming adept at marketing and managing credit cards.

Marks & Spencer have been particularly successful in retailer credit cards; they now have well over 1.5 million Chargecard holders, with sales accounting for as much as 12 per cent of their UK turnover.

## The management of credit

But the skills which retailers are learning in the management of credit are only just beginning, argues Steve Worthington; "there is undoubted potential", he writes, "for retailer credit cards to move on up into the relatively untapped market for the provision of financial services".

And what about EFTPoS? It seems unlikely, writes Eric Foster and Martin Houghton, that EFTPoS will lead to a cashless society. They take the view that it is much more probable that EFTPoS will take its place alongside present methods of payment, and be used by the consumer as only one of an expanded range of options when paying for goods and services.

Steve Worthington is sceptical about EFTPoS. He points out that credit cardholders are becoming increasingly sophisticated in using the free credit period offered by the card, to defer the moment when they actually have to part with the cash. Some 40 per cent of cardholders take advantage of the interest-free period. Why should those customers who use the free credit period relinquish that financial benefit by adopting the EFTPoS system?

And precisely *where* are shoppers spending all that money they've borrowed? Much less in the High Street and far more out-of-town. Russell Schiller, writing on the exodus out-of-town, draws attention to one of the more striking phenomena of the retail sector over the past few years — the development of the out-of-town shopping centre. Between 1980-84, he writes, total shopping centre floor space in the pipeline remained constant at around 30 million sq ft. By the end of 1986 it had risen to 100 million sq ft. The number of out-of-town regional shopping centres proposed of over 500,000 sq ft had risen from one in early 1984 to some 40 by the end of 1986.

Out-of-town shopping *per se* is not, of course, necessarily undesirable, but what is worrying, not only to Russell Schiller but to a number of other commentators, is the lack of a coherent planning policy which will take account both of the economic and social arguments which favour out-of-town shopping and the pressing need, at the same time, to preserve the High Street and to fight the problems of inner city decay.

Things are planned better on the continent, in Russell Schiller's view. "The somewhat weak and confused planning response to . . . decentralisation is a far cry from the confident days of the post-war years", he writes. "It is also a far cry from the experience of most of our continental neighbours, who have managed to achieve a more consistent policy on the ground with as rich a town planning tradition as Britain enjoys".

Town centres must improve their environmental quality to meet out-of-town competition. And Russell Schiller suggests pedestrianisation as the single most effective way of doing this. The UK is far behind the continent, especially Germany, in pedestrianisation schemes.

But deciding whether to put your shop in an out-of-town centre or in the High Street is only a beginning, according to David Rogers who writes about shop location methods. He's critical of retailers in this regard; "Retailers must be more thorough and organised about location procedures", he says. "Many have, but too many are still 'winging it'." He particularly deplores the initial unsophisticated stages of site-screening; "Is Hartlepool as nice as Wilmslow?" he cites as the sort of question too often heard around the board-room table. And he describes himself as "dumbfounded" to hear one major UK retailer say "that a day trip is sufficient field time to evaluate an investment decision that might average £6 million per store for that retailer!"

The question of physical distribution is another factor in determining location. Tony Rudd points out that management's grasp of "total distribution" strategies has improved over the past few years — strategies which combine all the individual elements of materials handling, storage and transport into a fully integrated logistics concept. And he suggests that a more professional approach is now emerging with the setting up, by the National Materials Handling

Centre, of an M.Sc. course in Distribution Technology and Management, in order to develop distribution specialists with a comprehensive depth of technical knowledge.

Another rapidly developing feature of British retailing over the past decade has been the convenience store. It can be seen as part of the polarisation process, with increasing emphasis on the massive superstore and the out of town shopping centre, as we have noted, and the rise of the small retailer at the other end of the spectrum. David Kirby, in his chapter on C-stores, points particularly to the role of the oil companies, who are beginning to recognise the potential for forecourt trading and to follow their counterparts overseas.

## The divided nation

But he points to another reason why the C-store has developed rapidly in the 1980s, and this is the emergence of the "divided nation". Increased unemployment, early retirement and an ageing population has created a large market segment consisting of relatively money-poor, time-rich consumers. Their shopping behaviour is characterised by small, individual, value for money purchases — they are natural C-store customers.

For in the end we come back to the consumer, and Michael Poynor charts the revolutionary changes that have been happening to that strange animal in the 1980s. The nuclear family, which we used to hear so much about — that cosy unit of Dad and a non-working Mum, plus two children — has given way to the vast and growing army of the singles, the separated, single-parent families, widowed, and divorced. Mr and Mrs Average are virtually extinct; two-person households can mean anything from double-earner Yuppie couples to partners on the dole.

The "two nation" syndrome can be identified through every level. In June 1986 the Child Poverty Action Group estimated "below the breadline" numbers to have increased from 6 million in 1979 to 9.3 million today. But many more families enjoy two cars, two TVs, and the doubtful pleasure of a hefty mortgage.

And what of employment policies? It has to be said this is one of the weakest areas of retail management; the EDC for the Distributive Trades in its 1985 report pinpointed a number of serious deficiencies. There are still limited management opportunities for women, still inadequate training provision overall, and more than a degree of scepticism about the Youth Training Scheme. Above all, and again as the EDC points out, average earnings in the retail trade have been, and remain among the lowest in the economy. Low pay makes a shabby basis for record profits.

But to end on a upbeat note — last word to Monty Lewis, who pinpoints what he describes as "one of the most important developments in the 1980s — that retailing is no longer regarded as a second class occupation". In his chapter on training and education, he notes that graduates are becoming more and more important in distribution; they are interested now in retailing as their first choice, not because they have been unsuccessful in alternative career choices. With the UK economy now strongly based on the service industries sectors, retailing and its links with the leisure industry is now a fashionable choice of career. And that surely is a promising sign for the future.

Nothing remains but to express heartfelt thanks to all those contributors who gave generously of their time to help create this book.

# The fashion revolution

Penelope Ody

*The fashion revolution is often said to have started with the advent of Next, but in fact the 25-plus woman customer was established as a key target before this. Next's contribution was to formalise and exploit the idea of niche marketing brilliantly, whilst Burton exemplified the "multi-strategy approach", with different companies within the group aiming at different market segments. Now the trend is towards local customer profiles; if the past decade has concentrated on lifestyle merchandising, perhaps the next will see a shift to localisation instead?*

Towards the end of 1981 the then highly traditional men's wear chain Hepworth appeared to commit a great folly. The company paid £1.75 million — some 50% over book value — to buy the ailing 79-outlet strong Kendall women's wear chain from Combined English Stores.

Hepworth remained non-committal about its plans for the chain and interest in the company, and its possible expansion beyond the conventional men's outerwear market, soon waned. So in spring 1982 when Hepworth re-launched the Kendall chain as Next few people in the fashion world had any inkling that women's wear retailing would never be the same again.

The basic Next concept was, admittedly, not new. Leading fashion retailers and suppliers had been talking about "lifestyle" merchandising for years with well co-ordinated collections targeted at specific market segments. What were new, however, were prices pitched strictly at Marks & Spencer's levels, a limited merchandise mix which made selection ultra-simple for the shopper, and a stylish store design guaranteed to appeal to the chain's target 25-plus customer.

George Davies, Next's originator, had also correctly judged the changing nature of the fashion shopper. While the '60s and '70s were decades when youth "ruled OK", by the 1980s the post-war baby boom generation had grown up and its women were complaining of the lack of suitable shops. Between the *avant-garde* appeal of Top Shop and the cosy classic comfort of Marks & Spencer, there was — in 1982 — a very apparent gap only partially filled by independent specialists, department stores and a few embryonic chains.

It is worth remembering, however, that this 25-plus customer was established as a key target shopper well before the arrival of Next and from the late 1970s onwards fashion suppliers had been pitching increasingly aggressively for her business. While it is easy to date the start of the revolution in high street fashion to the advent of Next, the foundations had been laid some time before then.

But while Jaeger, Mondi or Options (launched by Austin Reed in 1980 for the 30-plus "working woman or executive wife") had by 1982 brought exactly the same sort of Next formula to what the trade delights in calling the "better-end" of the "25-plus working woman" sector, Next applied it to the mass market and came up with a winner.

Almost overnight, Next appeared to transform shopping patterns: it also became an instant cult. Outlets were forced to close as the crush of customers built up or else ran out of stock and Next clones began to proliferate as other retailers sniffed success and leapt unashamedly onto the bandwagon. Yet, Next has proved to be much more than a nine-day wonder. In 1982/83 profits for the Hepworth group stood at £8.6 million, for 1986/87 they were £30.1 million (although around half of this was due to the acquisition of mail order firm, Grattan) and the Hepworth name has long since been replaced by the Next banner. Indeed, in May 1987 the wheel neatly turned full circle with a £325 million takeover by Next of Combined English Stores — the one-time parent of the original Kendall chain.

As is well-known Next has followed its success in women's wear with a men's wear chain, home furnishings, cosmetics, accessories, lingerie and children's wear. Each additional product launch has been geared to the same type of archetypal Next customer as the original women's wear chain. However, one only has to spend a short time in a typical Next shop to realise that customers spread well beyond the target 25-45 working women group. Women from late teens to late sixties can be seen in Next fashions underlining the fact that "lifestyle" really has very little to do with age and much more to do with attitudes and aspirations.

Yet, despite its undoubted influence, Next remains a comparatively minor player in the high street fashion game. In sales terms Marks & Spencer is still in the number one slot while Burtons — accounting for almost 5% of women's wear, according to Verdict Research — is at number two. Verdict puts C & A in third position with almost 4% of women's wear sales followed by BHS and Littlewoods.

With women's wear sales totalling nearly £6.4 billion in 1986, according to Textile Market Studies (compared with £4.6 billion in 1982) even these apparently insignificant market shares amount to very sizeable sums indeed.

But while Next has continued to diversify what has happened to the fashion revolution it heralded? With so many Next-like chains starting up in 1983/84 all aiming at the same hypothetical "25-plus working woman" it is not surprising that there have been casualties.

In 1982, for example, Raybeck was still attempting to make a success of its purchase of Bourne & Hollingsworth (renamed Bournes) buoyed by the success of its Lord John, Lady at Lord John and Werff fashion chains. By September 1985, after months of heavy losses it sold all 104 shops in these three chains to Next for £11.5 million and withdrew to consolidate its manufacturing base.

## Chains which folded

GUS launched Visuals in 1983 — only to quietly fold the chain three years later. And even Sir Terence Conran has had his problems with the fashion market although admittedly, with a chain aimed at quite a different lifestyle group. Now was launched by Mothercare in 1983 for the early teen market: it was closed down last year and many of the shops are now being transformed into the new Anonymous chain aimed at the 18-30 sector.

The first Anonymous shop opened in Hammersmith in November 1986 with Storehouse insisting there were no definite plans for expansion but by April 1987 seven more Anonymous outlets had opened.

The development is a joint venture between Storehouse and fashion manufacturers Melanie and Martin Lent of Pamplemousse (an *avant-garde* producer). According to Melanie Lent the Anonymous look is "young style with fine detail at affordable prices. It is for the individual who wants to create her own identity".[1]

Now traded at its peak from 30 outlets and while some of these have been converted to Mothercare shops several remain which could be used by Anonymous — clearly one of the new chains worth watching.

Anonymous also fills a different market niche to that taken by the successful Richards — Storehouse's revamped Richard Shops — chain which has been transformed into yet another multiple aiming at the 25-plus working woman. Indeed its very sales slogan "The working wardrobe" underlies this appeal with promotional material showing how the customer can wear her Richards' outfits for the office and then — with subtle variations — on to glamorous social events in the evening.

But while Next has certainly hogged the limelight in the past few years, there is no denying the success of Burton. The company would argue that it began the fashion revolution back in the 1970s: "I like to think that it started with Top Shop," Burton chairman Sir Ralph Halpern has said.[2]

Top Shop and its male equivalent Top Man, started life back in the swinging sixties and during the '70s were carefully repositioned to cater for specific target markets. Unlike Next with its 25-plus profile, Top Shop was and is geared to the high fashion trend market catering mainly for women in their late teens and early twenties with its small size Top Girl range taking the merchandise down to the 10-plus age group and Top Notch adding a little 25-plus sophistication. This mix was well-established before 1982 and has continued to develop along these lines.

In 1982, however, the main Burton vehicle for attracting the newly-emerging "25-plus working woman" market was Peter Robinson and the company had already begun to spread this chain beyond its flagship in London's Oxford Circus to Manchester, Croydon and Brent Cross. By early 1984 the company was predicting that Peter Robinson would grow to 250 outlets to cater for this demand.

Three years and the acrimonious Debenhams takeover battle later, Peter Robinson has faded back into history. Instead Burtons launched Principles in August 1984 as its answer to Next defining the target customer as the "25-45 woman who wants quality merchandise with style and service. A woman who wants perceived value."

Whether that woman failed to perceive the necessary value in Principles is debatable, but certainly the chain has not proved the phenomenal success of Next. However, Burton's performance in recent years has continued to impress. As already mentioned, Verdict Research estimates that Burton now accounts for almost 5% of UK women's wear sales and the group currently operates around 500 women's wear outlets and plans to open a further 650 over the next five years.

As well as Principles and Top Shop the women's wear outlets trade as Dorothy Perkins, Expressions and Evans. Expressions began as a forerunner to Principles aimed at a largely similar market although today it operates from only a handful of stand-alone shops and appears more successful as a business/formal wear range sold within Dorothy Perkins.

This chain has also been extensively re-targeted in the past few years moving from its traditional older-age/classic base to a younger fashion market and now apparently settling down with its 25/30-plus market and a merchandise mix that includes a highly successful range of maternity wear (a product group that would be totally out of place in Top Shop, for example). If the Principles customer is a working woman with aspirations, then Dorothy Perkins shoppers are more likely to be unwaged housewives with a more casual lifestyle.

During the Debenhams takeover battle in 1985, Sir Ralph Halpern commented that one reason for wanting the department store chain would be to take Burton into the 30-plus market and certainly the enlarged group now covers the entire fashion spectrum with individual labels aimed at almost every conceivable lifestyle segment. Debenhams had already gone some way along this segmentation route before the takeover and its then management were, understandably, far from pleased that during the acquisition battle their fashion marketing skills appeared to go unnoticed.

Debenhams had created its own special sections for the young/high fashion market (Just-In), it had a Next-style operation offering co-ordinated styles for the working woman (Accent) and it had a better end offer at the Jaeger market (Hyphen).

## Concession-type operations

Shortly after the Debenhams takeover, in autumn 1985, Burtons began opening Top Shop, Principles and Dorothy Perkins outlets as "concession-type" operations within its newly acquired department store chain. Arguably the result has been an over-proliferation of segmented ranges with considerable duplication in target markets and inevitably customer confusion.

Even so, one can see in the various Burton/Debenhams labels segmental merchandising philosophy very clearly at work.

Close inspection of customer profiles of many of today's women's wear chains may leave one with the impression that the female population is made up entirely of aspiring 25-45 year old career women firmly set on an upwardly mobile path. Nothing, of course, could be further from the truth as casualties among chains targeted at the market have shown.

But the past few years have also seen new launches aimed at both the high fashion 13-19 market and those with a more casual lifestyle.

A combination of declining population numbers in the teenage group and the serious problem of youth unemployment certainly caused a decline in this sector in the early 1980s. Snob, for example, had been one of the small-chain successes of the '60s and '70s but by 1983 its young market had changed to such an extent that the group went into receivership.

Similarly, chains like Miss Selfridge and Dorothy Perkins shifted to an older customer profile in line with current trends so inevitably a potential gap appeared in the market and new chains targeting at the early teen market — like the ill-fated Now development — began to appear.

Another of these — which also has its problems — is Surprise, launched in 1983 by a group of ex-Burtons directors and working on a high stockturn, short lead time and strong fashion message. Initially the chain appeared to go well with around 15 branches trading by 1985. However, by spring 1987 Surprise was down to four outlets and had converted the others to sweet shops.

Well-established chains like Chelsea Girl are successful, but the youth market, then, remains a problem area. There have been some success stories. Some 13 of the Snob shops were bought by fashion manufacturer Coutwell (which had failed in a £1 million bid to acquire the entire 24-strong chain) on the basis that if Snob closed completely then Coutwell would lose an important customer. By April 1987 the new owner was able to sell the now once again highly successful Snob chain to Etam for £5.4 million.

Etam regarded the acquisition as a useful means of filling a gap in its own lifestyle mix with Etam attracting 20-25-year olds and Tammy Girl appealing to the 8-12s market. Snob is seen as a useful vehicle aimed at the 13-19 sector.[3]

The acquisition is the first in Etam's 64-year history and the company has certainly proved to be one of the more enduring success stories of the '80s going public in 1984 and with profits up from £8.6 million in 1984/85 to £12.3 million in 1986/87. Again, although Etam's marketing argument is couched largely in age groups rather than lifestyle definitions this is best regarded as a convenient short-hand to describe target markets and is only part of the total picture.

But if the youth market remains a problem area other retailers have had more success with the casual sector. Phase 8, for example, which started with one shop in Wandsworth in the early 1980s now has some 10 outlets in London and a thriving wholesale operation with clothes aimed at what one might call stylish 25-plus non-working women.

Equally successful is the Dash operation started by clothing manufacturer Ellis & Goldstein in 1983. The company was best known then for its Eastex and Dereta collections with Eastex aimed at the 50-plus customer and Dereta targeting at shoppers only a few years younger. Dash was a complete contrast with casual co-ordinated merchandise sourced in the Far East. Like Eastex and Dereta, Dash started life as a concession operation in department stores although by November 1984 its first stand-alone shop opened.

Target customers initially were women between 20 and 45 although in practice the company was soon reporting a predominance of shoppers in their 30s and it wasn't long before Dash expanded into men's and children's wear as well. By 1985 there was even a Dash range of bedlinen launched by J P Stevens to match the Dash colour palette.

## Boom time for jogging

It was of course a boom time for jogging and tracksuits and Dash's casual but stylish image caught this lifestyle mood perfectly: not surprisingly its first stand-alone shop was in Brighton — home of healthy living and sporty lifestyles.

Although Dash merchandise is still very casual the company has responded well to subtle changes in its market and today there is less emphasis on sweatshirts and jogging suits with styles that are slightly smarter and more tailored.

The company is still firmly based in department stores, too, with a total of 121 women's wear concessions, eight stand-alone shops and six franchises.

A factor in Dash's success has clearly been its wide customer profile and the dangers of over-segmentation are apparent. Typical victim of this syndrome was the La Mama maternity wear franchise operation. The target customer here could perhaps crudely be described as the pregnant yuppy — affluent career women who needed smart maternity clothes and were happy to pay high prices for them. Unfortunately, as the franchisees found to their cost such women are few and far between, outside a few central urban areas and La Mama failed ignominiously at the end of 1986.

No examination of the women's wear scene could, of course, be complete without mention of Laura Ashley. The company predates the Next era, starting in 1953 in the legendary Pimlico attic where Mrs Ashley began printing her teatowels. There are now around 80 shops in the UK and although the company began long before the age of market segmentation its "sloane ranger" image — both for clothing and furnishings — has made the firm almost a byword for merchandise aimed at this sector: indeed, its outlets were originally in such ABC1 enclaves as Oxford, Bath, Harrogate or Cheltenham (as well as Sloane Street).

Unlike the other companies we have considered, Laura Ashley manufactures all its clothing lines and well over 50% of the merchandise is exported. The firm is thus very atypical of the fashion scene. Its styling has a distinctive handwriting often quite at variance with mainstream fashion trends. However, among many consumers Laura Ashley dresses remain *de rigueur* — and will no doubt continue to do so for many years to come.

Other women's wear manufacturers are also exploiting the retail route. Jaeger recently announced that it was closing its wholesale operations and in future would sell only through its own outlets, while in July Alexon announced plans for new stand-alone shops and concessions taking its number of outlets to over 200 worldwide.

Although the prime focus of the '80s fashion revolution has been the high street chains, similar lifestyle approaches have also been taken by the department stores — not always successfully.

Debenhams, as discussed earlier, had produced an enormous variety of own-label ranges aimed at different types of customers and House of Fraser has obviously been experimenting with lifestyle collections since Way In was launched at Harrods in 1967.

During the early-1980s House of Fraser introduced an enormous variety of own-label ranges aimed at various target markets. There was Weekender, for example, for the working woman at play; Additions as an up-market formal wear range; Lifestyle as a total concept for the fashion oriented 15-25 shopper and Innuendo as a specialised lingerie range of the teen market. There was also the umbrella Allander label for all sorts of own-brand lines and House of Fraser Exclusive as a top-end marque for limited high fashion lines.

Variety chains Littlewoods and BHS (in its pre-Storehouse days) also experimented with a variety of lifestyle labels which seem to have had only a transient existence on the shelves.

In contrast Marks & Spencer has remained faithful to St Michael — although its women's wear has changed dramatically since the arrival of Next. During 1983/84 M & S found its women's clothing sales slipping for perhaps the first time in its history and responded by completely revamping its presentation and merchandise mix. Out went the gondolas of neatly stacked knitwear and in came full colour posters of models in the latest styles, hanging rail presentation and clothes geared to a much more fashion conscious shopper.

In 1983 few "aspiring 25-plus working women" would have dreamed of buying a business suit from M & S, today many thousands do just that.

While Marks & Spencer is loath to admit to any outside influence in its changing philosophy (one director remarked somewhat disparagingly a few years back that Next's clothing sales couldn't even match M & S's cream cake business in terms of turnover) it has clearly seen which way the fashion wind is blowing in the high street and trimmed its sales accordingly.

Stand-alone lingerie and fashion outlets have been opened and co-ordinates are now well presented Next-style in M & S stores. The company's booming sales figures testify to the success of this move with clothing sales up 10% in real terms for 1986/87, pre-tax profits of £432 million and the company claiming a 16% slice of UK clothing sales.

## M & S fights back

Marks & Spencer has certainly succeeded in attracting the higher-spending younger customer back to its stores but at what price? Its suppliers have certainly been put under considerable pressure to produce shorter runs of more fashionable merchandise at minimum prices (and falling profits among many of these suppliers in recent years bear witness to their difficulties in fulfilling these demands.[4] In addition the traditional "classic" shopper (generally the 45-plus customer) has to some extent been alienated by the developments and stores like John Lewis and Debenhams (in pre-Burton days) reported booming sales of Marks & Spencer-style basic knitwear and separates to these customers.

A problem with many lifestyle ranges remains that in the confusion of the fashion floor the target customer often fails to appreciate that the range had been designed specifically for her.

In the days before the Burton takeover, Debenhams was actually running a major training programme for its sales staff which included sessions on lifestyle merchandising designed to help the assistants understand the concepts behind labels like Hyphen and Just-In and match these more effectively to their customers. If sales staff are confused by the lifestyle concepts then one can be certain that Mrs Average Shopper trying to find a blouse usually fails to appreciate the subtle differences of, for example, an Additions or Allander label.

While lifestyle merchandising may be ideal in theory, unless the store makes a real effort to get the total concept and image across to the customer (as Next does so successfully) then the label becomes just an insignificant and irrelevant name.

Perhaps it is not surprising that House of Fraser's new chairman and chief executive Brian Walsh recently said in an interview that the company was: ". . . definitely winding down on in-house merchandising programmes. We went overboard on our own-label merchandise. But for department stores you are better off sticking to manufacturer's brand names — people expect to find them there."[5]

This move away from own-label runs quite *contra* to developments in the early part of the decade. According to TMS, for example, the own-label share of sales in multiple women's wear outlets increased from around 30% in 1979 to 65% in 1984.[6] Much of this private branding focused on new lifestyle collections. The new philosophy at House of Fraser is a distinct movement away from this trend and one which could typify changing attitudes to lifestyle merchandising as retailers develop more sophisticated marketing techniques. Lifestyle merchandising is — after all — a very "broad brush" approach to selling, greatly over-simplifying a store's customer profile. Using ACORN or Pinpoint techniques a store can now more closely identify its exact types of customers and tailor the merchandise mix more closely to their needs.

Interestingly, this is just the sort of approach taken by the highly successful Italian chain, Benetton. Here franchisees are able to tailor the product mix to match their particular local customer profile. Benetton's corporate promotions concentrate on getting across a young, colourful, fashionable image, but the actual product mix varies enormously between stores. Sophisticated manufacturing techniques which rely on garment dyeing are at the heart of this approach.[7]

**Table 1: some of the new fashion chains launched in recent years**

| Name | Parent group | Target age | Launch date | No of outlets a |
|------|-------------|-----------|-------------|-----------------|
| Anonymous | Storehouse plc/ Pamplemousse | 18-30 | April 1987 (pilot October 1986) | 7 |
| Benetton | Franchise operation of Italian Benetton group | 15-30+ | Italy in 1968 UK approx 1978 | 280 in the UK |
| Experience | Burton Group plc | 25-45 | Late 1983 | 5 b |
| Next | Hepworth (now Next plc) | 25-45 | Spring 1982 | 314 c |
| Now | Storehouse plc | 10-19 | Spring 1983 | d |
| Options | Austin Reed | 30+ | 1980 | 37 e |
| Principles | Burton Group plc | 25-45 | August 1984 | 140 |
| Richards | Storehouse plc | 25-45 | f | 160 |
| Solo | Paul Poly (a clothing firm) | 18-30 | November 1984 | 20 |
| Surprise | | 12-20 | July 1983 | 4 |
| Visuals | GUS | 25-45 | Autumn 1982 | g |

a Approximate figures for August 1987.
b Expressions sections are also included in almost all 370 Dorothy Perkins outlets.
c Divided between 107 Next-Too shops. 150 Next Collection and 57 lingerie outlets. Next acquired the 200-strong Paige fashion in the CES deal and will use 40 for end-of-line cleaning operations, 40 will be closed and the remaining 120 split between the mainstream Next businesses.
d Folded October 1986 and its 30 outlets transferred to Mothercare, Richards and Anonymous.
e All within branches of Austin Reed.
f Formerly Richard Shops acquired by Storehouse in late 1983 from UDS. 200 outlets are scheduled to be trading by the end of 1987.[9]
g Folded 1985.

Equally pertinent is a comment made by George Davies: "We're beginning to get a feel for the local differences, " he said, "In future we may have a core range and then vary the rest of the collection depending on the location of the outlet."[8]

To some extent this is already happening with the Next-Too and Next Collection ranges aiming at slightly different market levels and offering a degree of exclusivity.

Perhaps if the past decade has been one of lifestyle merchandising in the fashion sector, the next will be a shift to localisation instead?

## References

1. *Drapers Record,* April 4, 1987. See also *Marketing* November 27, 1986.
2. Quoted in "Fashion retailing — what next?", *Retail & Distribution Management,* September/October 1984, page 9.
3. *Fashion Weekly,* April 30, 1987, page 1.
4. *Women's Fashions,* published by Key Note Publications, 2nd Edition 1986, page 27.
5. Quoted in *Men's Wear,* April 2, 1987.
6. Roy Holliss, "The changing marketplace in fashion," *Retail & Distribution Management,* January/February 1986, page 12.
7. "Could the Benetton star shine brighter?", *Marketing Week,* July 4, 1986, pages 30-36.
8. "Next — now for the interior," *Retail & Distribution Management,* September/October, 1985, page 21.
9. *Fashion Weekly,* April 2, 1987.

# The strategic significance of design

Rodney Fitch & James Woudhuysen
*Fitch & Co*

*Design has long since ceased to be a merely decorative function. In retailing, it is now recognised as an essential part of the merchandising policy. The new "niche" retailers of the 80s rely heavily on good design for instant customer identification and appeal.*

14

$A$t Fitch we work with clients to ensure that, alongside marketing and finance, design becomes a strategic business resource — that it is brought in at the start of every decision-making process involving expansion. In this chapter, we want to explain why the function of design is not purely decorative but, in management terms, highly practical and commercial.

In the best companies, design resources are managed with all the seriousness shown in marketing or finance. At Fitch, we believe that good and bad designs are not just matters of opinion, but can and should be measured and accountable. Consultants outside the realm of design may deliver a hard-pressed retail management endless reports; but a good designer will deliver a working, exciting store that directly conveys his client's management philosophy.

As retail designers, our point of departure is the customer. What goes on in his or her head? Is the customer more attracted to watching tonight's television than to late-night shopping?

Design is about capturing the consumer's imagination. Through this, the consumer's time and his disposable income is captured. Design thus deals in the issues which come closest to a human being's personal reality. Designing is about needs and desires, about social circumstances; it is about touching people in their hearts as well as in their pockets.

To master the realities of customer preference, retail designers must try to be expert in their clients' present and future markets. But when they are good, their expertise is, while reliant on conventional market research, both broader and deeper than it. The reason is simple: we should be concerned with what people want, rather than just with what we can sell them. A good designer, therefore, will conduct a continuous international enquiry into the consumer's visual, tactile and spatial consciousness. That way, he can come up with the kind of design that will persuade tomorrow's consumer with substantial arguments — with feelings and motifs that will stand the test of time, that will stay relevant and contemporary.

Good design offers the retailer a strategic vantage point on the consumer. Its starting-point — people — is amply justified, for customers beget more people. In retail environments as elsewhere, people like to be where they can relate to each other, where they are stimulated, rather than bored, where they are satisfied rather than frustrated, where they find solutions rather than problems. They want to be understood, but not talked down to. Consumers are *not stupid;* they just want to be happy. The strategic role of the retail designer is to ensure that this wish is fulfilled.

There are three specially topical reasons why retailers need designers to play this 'advocate of the consumer' role:

In the past five years there has been a definite improvement in British consumer consciousness of design. This improvement applies both to Britain's ageing population, and to its youth. Today's older people stay younger for longer than was the case in the past. Their adult lives have generally been accompanied by rising standards of comfort, and they expect to benefit from the best kind of products and environments.

On the other hand, young people now have an instinctive sense of the mediocre, and will not stand for it. Teenagers debate style with fresh passion; adolescents are conscious of technological innovation as never before. Even infants and children today grow up to toys, schoolbooks, laboratories and sports equipment unprecedented in their sophistication and scope.

The consequences of this to architects and designers are immediate. Where the catchment area has a high incidence of children, as in new towns, shops and shopping centres should have special children's features, parent-and-baby rooms, crèches and the like. These features should perhaps have a limited lifespan, so that, as demographics change, play areas can become youth centres. On the other hand, more chairs will be necessary all over Britain, as customers age and so more frequently feel the need to sit down.

Then there is the question of consumer health and safety. The major international disasters of recent times are just the most vivid factors making health and safety a universal preoccupation. For retailers, this means that consumers now expect higher design standards in environments, product information and product reliability.

There has been a substantial shift by consumers away from

wanting a better standard of living towards wanting a better quality of life. This trend manifests itself in many ways, for example:
— consumers consistently want to trade up (even the less affluent want to do this)
— they are interested in environmental and product innovation
— they reject sterile architecture in general and high-rise flats in particular.

In addition, more and more people cry: "Don't regiment me. Don't institutionalise me. Treat me as an individual". One has only to observe personal fashion to see more obvious examples of this. Today's consumers take a more qualitative, more judgmental, more egocentric view than once they did.


## Shopping and leisure

What does this mean? Simply this: that, as people become more mobile, as their use of retail facilities moves away from necessity toward discretionary choice, design can help retailers create a powerful interface between shopping and *leisure*. It can make the act of purchasing blend with eating, drinking and being entertained — above all, with staying on the premises. In this way, what once were errands can turn into pleasurable visits.

The challenge, then, is for retailers to *use* design, not as a cosmetic, but to understand the individual within the community or the catchment area and to provide for his or her behavioural, aspirational and lifestyle needs.

Customers look for the right merchandise of the right quality at the right price. They look not just for the standard kind of products dispensed by big-brand multiples, but products with which they can express themselves. Often, such products are only available from local specialists — and it is just these specialists that need maximum support, financially and in terms of design.

In a shopping centre, therefore, we need a style of design which is compatible with tenant mix and market position; one which neither degrades quality merchandise nor accentuates cheapness; one which refuses to swamp local participation with national or international characteristics. In shops we cannot be satisfied simply with interior design for better layout, merchandising or stock allocation, nor even with signage, ticketing and packaging.

We must make certain that ranging and the choice of product

presented to the consumer are correct. At best, the retailer will ask the same group of designers not only to change his shells and his shelves, but also to make proposals to his suppliers about the kind of goods they put on those shelves. In short, retail designers should work in tandem with product and fashion designers and product technology and marketing specialists.

Too often the retailer's approach to his geographical location is on a par with a cavalier attitude to his wares. Yet it must be said that architects can be insensitive; they do tend to design things in their own image. Equally, however, developers do go round the world, picking up fashionable new ideas, and planners and local authorities do want the latest thing for their town. Everybody does his own thing and *hopes* that the customer end-user will grow to like it. The tendency is — design first, ask questions about who it's for only later.

Baltimore is a wonderful shopping centre development, but, as an inspiration to docklands opportunities in Britain, should not be slavishly copied. Equally, what works at Edmonton, Canada in shopping and leisure terms is not right necessarily in Edmonton, Middlesex.

Good design and architecture for shopping centres and shops is about that old-fashioned phrase 'fitness for purpose'. The purpose must be to provide the most appropriate and agreeable experience for both tenants and customers. Therefore, what is right for the US or Japan is not necessarily right for the UK or France. This applies regionally too. The Dordogne is not the Ruhr, Paris is not Vienna. In the UK the southeast is different from the west country. The needs of a cathedral city are different from those of a market town.

This diversity of need must be developed in, tenanted in and designed in. Properly differentiated, fit for purpose and harmonious, a well designed place will then give premium status not only to retailers and their products, but to people themselves. That is the only way they can be made to return again and again.

Once more, the consequences are practical. Shopping centres must provide meeting places, community news, local displays and neighbourhood events together with strong independent retailer representation. Regional centres must be places to have a day out in — that provide the very best of the traditional high street, all under one roof. Shops must have fascias which sit well with the rest of the streets, and must be built and fitted out with local materials whenever possible.

From stores, people demand more than just cheap prices. They are looking for value. Now, value has many dimensions; but since the lowest price can only belong to one trader, everybody else must use non-price factors to express their version of value. Here are two of the major non-price factors:

(i) *User friendliness and intelligibility.* In a world of denser and denser information, design can serve to unite and clarify the role of the different parts of a dispersed retail venture. It can identify the venture as a whole, act as a focus of its reputation, and sharpen its impact in the marketplace. For it to do this, design — especially graphic design — must make stores and merchandise presentation user-friendly and intelligible.

At Fitch we never forget that, in a competitive democracy, our customers and our clients have a choice. Today the retailer generally has one chance, and one alone, to pitch for the shopper's attention. Present a blurred or ambiguous message, or fall down with unclear names, typography or bannering, and that chance is lost.

(ii) *Stores are not just stores.* The concept that stores are there only for shopping is questionable. People come to stores not just to buy things, but to be informed and amused. Indeed, a recent survey of retail consumers in the US discovered that 'to buy something' was only sixth given in a list of reasons for being in a shopping environment. More important reasons were to mingle and to get ideas.

## Covent Garden

Once derelict, London's Covent Garden is now a shopping Mecca — not only for the shops, but for jugglers and the clowns. This confirms that the store operator must consider himself an impresario. He is in the business of theatre, or he is nothing.

Design can help to create a unique retail proposition. In the 1990s, the retail marketplace will grow increasingly polarised and competitive. To be a winner in this environment, the successful retailer will need to engage design in the following areas:

(i) *Differentiation.* Take British retail banking. With 6000 branches between them, most UK banks look exactly the same. Yet to distance oneself from the competition by product, environment and positioning is essential. Design is the outward signal of this. It keenly expresses management's desire to set its whole culture apart from that of its rivals.

Midland Bank has, with Fitch's help, begun to do just this in the UK. Our new branches express the Midland's difference from the other banks in the retail banking market. High tech equipment, such as ATMs, complements the personal service available — a combination which customers clearly find attractive. At present, we have started the redesign of 50 High Street outlets, following the success of our prototypes at Bristol.

(ii) *Focused retailing*. Design can help focus a retailer's market position. For example, the Burton Group is among Fitch's oldest and most design-aware clients. Since we started to work together in 1977, Burton has become the UK's most successful apparel retailer, with a national market share of nearly 10 per cent. This has been achieved by a commitment to focused retailing, expressed by design. Thus:

— Burton Menswear appeals to 25-40 year olds
— Top Man appeals to men in their twenties
— Top Shop is targeted at women between 15 and 25
— Principles, launched in 1983 to compete with Next, appeals to the more mature in the 25-40 year old market, among both men and women.

Each Burton subsidiary thus makes an unequivocal design statement within its market sector. Design is a key weapon with which to implement the basic strategy of market segmentation.

(iii) *Repositioning*. Design can help move customer perceptions. This is what we have begun to do for Debenhams, one of the UK's largest department store groups, acquired by our clients, the Burton Group, in 1985. We shall refurbish the entire chain, over 4.5 million square feet, by 1990. Our brief? To reposition this department store 'dinosaur' as a more efficient, more convenient, more exciting, glamorous place to shop.

(iv) *Stores as brands*. Strong retail brands are powerful factors in the shopping experience. Design can help support the brand. Indeed we need to think of stores, not just as so much property, but as brands which need constant support to keep their reputations high.

In a recent survey in the UK, we tried to identify some of the brands that were most 'front of mind' amongst a wide range of consumers. It was not surprising to discover that four of our leading retailers were in the top ten best brands. This is a powerful position, for brand reputation is all a retailer really has.

Consistently pursued, good design can carry a brand through any number of changes. It can be not only the physical, but also the spiritual and intellectual framework for presenting a retailer's corporate culture. Benetton is an international example of this. Who knows or cares where the factory is? This retail brand, like some packaged goods, transcends geographic boundaries.

Note that a strategic, design-based approach to stores as brands can impress corporate culture not only on customers, but also on staff — leading to higher productivity and morale, lower absenteeism, and higher, more committed standards of service.

For too long, traders have thought only in numerical terms; seldom have they thought in terms of the soul. Too many buildings, too many stores and too many developments deliberately try not to show wit or humour. Popular taste and culture has been derided as vulgar by architects and critics alike. Perhaps that is why so many stores and other public places have been built as temples to ordinariness.

This reserve must change. Articulate customers now look for more than just price shopping or comparative shopping. They look for pleasure and they look for hope. For them, design can often be the quickest way to the heart.

Design is a prime way of *communicating*. Design is sensory — people can touch it, feel it, experience it, criticise it. In other words, design talks to people. This is the ultimate strategic significance of design to modern retailing.

21

# EPoS and the Retailer's Information Needs

## Dr Gil Jones
*Chairman, RMDP*

*The last ten years or so have seen radical changes in the EPoS market. Recently we have witnessed a mushrooming of technological advances together with an increasing "softness" in the design and use of EPoS systems. There has also recently been the sudden emergence of a wide range of design and marketing initiatives — all of which make the subject of EPoS not only more exciting but also much more confusing.*

*This chapter takes the form of a guide through the labyrinth, identifying what should be the retailer's major concerns.*

E PoS (Electronic Point of Sale), the bringing of the computer right to the front of the shop operation, has been around both in concept and reality for a number of years now, so is a familiar subject. Nevertheless, this is a good time to review the subject because although EPoS systems and approaches have always been subject to rapid changes in design, what has happened in the last year or so puts all previous rates of change in the second division. EPoS could be argued to be passing through its second revolution — assuming you accept that the first one ever took place.

Why are retailers so pre-occupied with EPoS? Essentially this is because since time began they have grappled with the essential problem of knowing precisely what they sell, and what they have in stock, at a fine enough level of detail to take meaningful operational decisions. The majority of retailers carry the type of stock where keeping on top of this problem borders on the impossible. When EPoS came along they saw for the first time the possibility of solving the problem once and for all. And when you consider the almost vicious level of competition that has arisen in retailing today, it's easy to see why retailers want to steal a lead in this particular area.

It is often forgotten that the primary rationale for the introduction of EPoS, and all the investment and upheaval that it involves, is the solution of this very basic problem. But while the problem is simple in concept, it is immensely difficult in practical detail. After all, it is not enough to know that you are selling a lot of dresses, or even dresses of a particular style. It is necessary to know precisely which colour and which size is selling in which branch, and what the structure of the remaining stock is in these terms.

In constructing this review it is worth diverting for a moment to provide a little historical perspective. As I said earlier there is nothing new about the problem — only the solution. As early as the late 1960s, some of the more enterprising retailers were beginning to experiment with various forms of cash register that were capable of capturing very much more data about the transaction than just the price. Some of these, for example, wrote data onto punched paper tape which could be taken and read into a computer later.

These were the precursors of today's modern EPoS terminals. By the early to mid 1970s, EPoS in more or less the form we know it today had emerged, though in real terms these systems were enormously expensive and — since they were developed well before the microtechnology that we now take for granted — they were rigid in design and by modern standards extremely low in performance. (It is easy to forget that we didn't have electronic calculators until the early 1970s and the ones we did have, until Sinclair pulled his first major rabbit out of the hat, cost around £100 each).

In spite of these limitations certain retail sectors — cash and carry and department stores are examples — where particularly favourable cost benefit conditions existed, did invest quite heavily in EPoS.

The late '70s saw the emergence of the ROM-driven terminal-based systems which brought EPoS into the reach of the small retail outlet for the first time. The early '80s saw the first EPoS equipment influenced in design terms and cost microcomputer market, and as we have moved through the l have witnessed a mushrooming of technological advances hand in hand with an ever-increasing 'softness' in the design and use of these EPoS systems.

This whole design development pattern is a bit like a guided missile, taking off slowly, gathering speed in a specific direction, then finally hitting its target and 'splatting' out in all directions. What we have been witnessing in the last few months is the beginning of this final phase — the splatting out! We have seen the sudden emergence recently of a wide range of design initiatives — and marketing initiatives — that make the subject of EPoS at once much more exciting but also much more confusing.

These changes manifest themselves in a number of interesting ways. For example, if you look at the list of exhibitors at the 'EPoS' Congress, held in London each Autumn, and the primary exhibition dedicated to this specialism, you will see first of all that the number of exhibiting companies has more than doubled in the last two years and also — unless you are extremely well informed — that there are companies present that you have never heard of. Equally, the shortlists of potential EPoS systems suppliers that are going up for consideration to the boards of leading retail organisations are unrecognisable compared with similar shortlists a year or two ago. We have new companies, with new approaches, in some extremely unfamiliar corporate groupings.

One of the main reasons why this has come about is a recognition (at last) that retailers are not actually interested in EPoS at all, they are only interested in solving the problems that EPoS is designed to solve. Elementary though this may seem, it has taken quite a long time for the message to be received and understood throughout the industry. One of the immediate and obvious effects of this is to throw up a plethora of software led solutions where the retailer is offered software packages that are designed to process the detailed data captured in the shop into meaningful and actionable reports. The device to capture the data at the front end of this process — the EPoS terminal — is then considered, but many of these software packages can operate with data from a number of different EPoS terminals and systems so the actual choice of the EPoS system becomes relatively important.

## Multi-supplier approaches

This is leading to retailers being specifically offered solutions from multiple suppliers who are co-operating together to present a unified solution. This contrasts with the situation a short while ago where multi-supplier approaches tended to be discouraged. Quite commonly now companies traditionally involved in different parts of the market — backroom computers, shop-based computers and equipment, software, communications — combine, either within a formal corporate grouping or through some marketing agreement, to work together in presenting a solution to a specific problem.

There is also a significant shift in attitudes regarding the role of EPoS in the retail environment, and this is bringing with it an extension in the use of the data collected by the EPoS terminals into a wide range of areas that go well beyond the straightforward stock control issue. This is important, economically if for no other reason. EPoS systems do not come cheap and the data they collect can clearly have an importance in the retail organisation in many areas. Whilst retailers — even some of the large household name ones — have not yet conquered the really basic problem of making sure that the right stock is in the right place at the right time, they nevertheless have a strong incentive to move beyond this and improve their information systems in a wide variety of other areas.

So EPoS is beginning to be seen — rightly — as merely the starting point in the whole retail information system cycle and a whole string of further application areas are beginning to emerge and be successfully applied.

Some of the examples are particularly exciting. Space management allows the retailer to measure the relationship between the amount of space given to particular lines of merchandise against their rate of sale. This can be linked with Direct Product Profitability (DPP), if desired, to encompass not just straight stockturn rate but also the precise contribution to the company's 'bottom line' of each line of merchandise. In this way it is possible to tailor displays to reflect more precisely the strengths and weaknesses of particular merchandise lines and couple this again with customer demand.

These techniques, through the use of microcomputers and advanced graphics, can allow the merchandiser the facility to contrast the economic issue of contribution versus display space with the aesthetic issue of the visual display itself. With some systems it is possible, once the ideal display has been arrived at in Direct Product Profitability terms, to switch to video mode and display on the same screen a simulated video picture of what the display in that form would look like.

This move toward the more total information system approach shows up clearly also in the increasing interest being shown by retailers, and consequently by those responsible for supplying software and hardware systems to the retailer, in Decision Support Systems. This is the rather general title given to systems which take the basic raw data from fundamental sources such as EPoS and process it into tabular and graphical report structures that assist the retail manager to take the essential decisions that routinely have to be taken in the operation of the retail organisation.

This is best illustrated by example: there are packages available now that use this type of approach to provide a fully integrated financial and merchandise unit planning system for the retailer. This again is one of the traditionally difficult areas for the retailer to crack, so such systems are genuinely attractive.

Imagine a retailer who operates a hundred branches with a number of merchandise departments within each. For each season it is necessary to construct a set of plans that will ensure that each branch has sufficient merchandise within each merchandise department to meet its forecasted sale in that area. This is an immensely complex reiterative problem that every retailer has had sleepless nights over. Changes in forecasted sales for the whole company, or branch by branch, will affect every other part of the equation, and it is necessary to ensure that the financial forecasts can be transalated into workable merchandise unit terms. Decision support systems structures allow this to be carried out readily, drawing on data files constructed from sales history and worked on relatively low cost microcomputer power.

## Good application software

This increased emphasis on software in the design and application of EPoS systems has itself brought about some interesting developments. For a start there is a lot more good quality application software coming onto the market in the form of software packages designed to assist with particular applications in the retail sector. Some of these have been described above but of course there are many more, and there is also more and more software designed to help retailers of specific types. This latter point is important since the needs of a retail pharmacy bear little comparison with those of a fast food restaurant or a video hire outlet.

This development is most welcome: one of the main criticisms of earlier EPoS systems and their suppliers was that the hardware in question — albeit very good hardware in some cases — was dumped onto the market without adequate associated software, leaving the retailer to sort this problem out for himself by whatever means he could. Since retail managers are not used to buying cars without engines, this approach brought a lot of genuine criticism to the equipment supplier industry. Now things are at last improving, though there still are problems.

Looked at from the standpoint of the suppliers of EPoS equipment and associated services, this application software question is a difficult one. You can supply the equipment without software, saying that you will develop software to meet an individual customer's requirements, but this solution is both slow and expensive. It also means you have to secure the initial order on a promise. Alternatively, you can develop specific packages and market these with the equipment. Inevitably with this approach the package won't be quite right and it will need some modification, sometimes

27

extensive, which is clearly undesirable.

There is also the problem that to be truly effective the package needs to be fairly specific to an individual application, and possibly to a highly specialised type of retail operation, so the total market for the package may be quite limited (compared, for example, to the mass market available for a spreadsheet package or a payroll package).

To get round this problem suppliers are moving toward the use of advanced programming techniques. They are doing this in search of a method that will allow them to start from a basic software shell and rapidly (and cheaply) tailor this into a powerful package for a particular user application. The approach being taken by many suppliers for this is via the use of fourth generation languages (4GL's) and associated program generation techniques. A fourth generation language is essentially a higher level language than those normally used which allows certain functions needed by the user to be provided for with one or two simple instructions within the language.

A crude analogy is the 'circle' instructions available on some domestic microcomputers. The use of this button allows the user to draw a circle on the screen: he can do this because the use of the button calls into play a whole complicated piece of program logic, or algorithm, that has been previously written and installed in the computer's memory. You can imagine having a series of instructions of this type within a fourth generation language developed specifically for retailing, so that, say, causing the system to look up a price in a price look-up function can be set up via a single, simple, instruction.

This whole approach is gaining ground and can be expected to make quite a major impact over the next 2-3 years on the ways in which retail systems are designed and used.

Before leaving the general subject of EPoS systems design, we ought to mention the importance of the personal computer. We touched on this earlier: basically EPoS systems design has followed a path that closely parallels that of the personal computer all throughout the 1980s, and is continuing to do so. This is hardly surprising. After all, EPoS systems have in common with the personal computer that they are essentially distributed systems, they need to be cheap and reliable and they are frequently operated by people with little or no formal training. Therefore they must be fairly 'bulletproof'.

The merging of these two design cultures is not difficult to detect. A walk round the 'EPoS' Congress exhibition will reveal the simple fact that almost every stand, whatever the exhibitor is selling or whatever slant he may be taking, will have personal computers on it performing one role or another. The range of these roles is also quite interesting: personal computers are used in small retail organisations as computers in their own right, paralleling the more powerful equipment used by larger organisations.

They are also used in many retail situations dedicated to specific tasks such as pre-processing of information, control of communications, control of EPoS terminals within a medium sized store. On top of this, they may be used as intelligent terminals, allowing retail managers to investigate the information held within the retail system, and of course they are used by retailers in all of the normal business applications that would apply to any organisation — word processing, financial planning, etc. A number of retail organisations are in fact moving toward paper-free systems altogether; in these circumstances personal computers, hooked up to the retail information system, would be used by all levels of operations management to obtain the information that they would previously have received through written reports. Examples here include merchandisers and buyers, warehouse/depot managers, and many more.

## The issue of standardisation

A related issue that has to be close to the retailer's heart is that of standardisation. Retailers, in common with any user groups, will benefit from standardisation in all areas. By way of example the establishment of universally agreed standards in communications protocols would lead to a situation where the equipment supplied by one manufacturer could more easily be joined together and used in conjunction with that supplied by another. This equipment might include EPoS terminals, in-store micros, or whatever. While the situation in this area is improving, it is still not yet quite that easy, which leads to a state of affairs where a retail organisation might find itself trapped within the clutches of their existing supplier, or unable to shop around to get the best type of equipment to solve a particular problem.

An example of how the successful establishment of international standards can help is to be found in the area of merchandise coding.

The emergence of the UPC (Universal Product Code) in the USA during the 1970s, and its expression in the form of a bar code, led the way for an extension of this code in the form of the EAN (European Article Numbering) code becoming a truly international standard. This brought in its wake significant benefits, initially in the supermarket area where laser scanners reading the EAN bar codes have overcome the previously insuperable problem of recording in detail sales of the high volume/low value merchandise transacted in that environment. The standardisation has also brought significant reductions in equipment prices and improvements in the technology involved, particularly in the printing of the bar codes.

Success in this area has in turn influenced retailers of other types: department stores worldwide have decided that this is a tide they should swim with rather than against, and have abandoned their earlier endorsement of OCR marking techniques in favour of an extension in the use of EAN codes. Boots, in the pharmacy area, and W H Smith in the books/periodicals area (both organisations grappling with the high volume/low value problem) have further boosted the adoption of EAN into a string of other product areas, so we are now seeing the emergence of the EAN system as a truly universal code covering all merchandise types (or virtually all) in almost every major retail trading country.

Following on the back of this success, the Article Number Association in the UK has turned its gaze towards solving another nutty little problem — that of communications between the retailer and his merchandise supplier. Their initiative here has led to the standardisation of invoice and delivery note formats under a set of standards called Tradacoms: this is now leading to the possibility of communications between retailers and their supplier organisations being carried out on a computer to computer basis, cutting enormously the timescales and costs involved.

There is one important area that has so far escaped the good intentions of all concerned in regard to the establishment of universal standards. This is the area of automated payments, and more particularly EFTPoS (Electronic Funds Transfer at the Point of Sale). However, this is the specialised subject of another essay within this work, so I can safely leave this little bag of worms in the very capable hands of my co-authors.

Before concluding, it would be sensible to take a glance at the EPoS situation from a total market standpoint. The actual market penetration of EPoS within the UK retail sector is still quite low — around 10 per cent overall, measured in terms of the percentage of cash points that could be argued to fall within the potential market for some kind of EPoS terminal that have actually already undergone conversion to this technology. However, this penetration rate is rising quite quickly, particularly in certain sectors, such as the larger supermarkets and the speciality multiples. In some sectors penetration is already high — we mentioned earlier department stores and cash and carry outlets.

## EPoS is big business

These facts, taken together with the recognition that traditional retailing in the UK has a turnover of some £90 billion, to which must be added a further massive turnover from what we call quasi retail restaurants, fast food outlets, travel agents, etc — means that by any standards when talking EPoS we are talking big business. Retailers spend on average around 1 per cent of their gross turnover on information systems, so a simple calculation will tell you why there are so many companies vying for market share in this area and why there are ever more companies seeking to jump aboard this particular bandwagon.

The important thing from the retailers' point of view must be that the systems he is purchasing have been properly researched and carefully designed to meet his needs and are supported by a company that has the financial and operational resources to ensure that they can be installed and operated successfully in his organisation. Whilst the majority of companies offering systems and services to retailers qualify soundly in these areas, there are nevertheless others who need to be weeded out or watched very carefully, and we would strongly recommend retailers moving forward with investments in this area to ensure, by whatever means, that they are fully briefed and extremely well informed before they proceed.

So . . . in conclusion. The retailer must take the broader view in approaching the whole question of in-store retail systems, and EPoS in particular, looking first at his overall information system and information needs, then seeing how the benefits of EPoS along with a number of other important approaches, fits into this total picture. This should lead to a much more balanced outlook than has been exhibited by many retailers in the past and should also lead to a number of shifts of emphasis. For example, most retailers will probably spend more on software than they originally expected, and equivalently less on hardware. They may end up with totally different types of management reports, possibly not on paper at all and perhaps using advanced computer graphics techniques. They may buy equipment from companies — perhaps working in conjunction with others — that initially they had never heard of.

The important thing is to achieve a system which exhibits genuine flexibility — not possible even a short time ago, and which embodies a value for money characteristic that may very favourably surprise. In any case, no retailer should go ahead until he has carried out a cost benefit calculation that satisfies himself and his board regarding the wisdom of going ahead. This calculation will almost certainly prove extremely difficult — it may border on the impossible — but it is an important discipline, and must be done.

Many retailers will have the people within their organisation with the experience, knowledge and time successfully to carry out the precursory investigations that are essential before taking on board such an important change. If not, then it is important to pull in those skills from the outside on a temporary basis. The cost of this, though it may be fairly high, will be a lot less than getting this one wrong.

# The Credit Explosion

Steve Worthington
*University of Stirling*

*Credit is no longer discreditable; we are all borrowers now. The credit explosion sparked off first the growth of bank credit cards and then the development of retailer credit cards. Success stories amongst these include Marks & Spencer, Burton, and Storehouse. Retailers such as these are becoming skilled in the management and marketing of credit.*

# The Changing Face of British Retailing

$H$igh street sales showed every sign of breaking records in the summer of 1987 as easy credit and reduced mortgage payments increase spending power and the tourist industry picks up. Retailers were generally optimistic about their prospects for 1987 and the retail sector continues to attract favourable comment from the city.

The current consumer boom is fuelled by high real income growth (for those of us fortunate enough to be in employment) and a willingness by consumers to borrow large amounts of money. 1986 saw a rise of 14% in the amount of outstanding consumer credit, more than three times the rise in prices and double the rise in earning. Department of Trade and Industry figures showed that the amount of credit advanced during May 1987 was at a level of £3.04 billion. The May figure takes the total advances over the latest three month period 11% higher than in the previous three months.

The attitude to borrowing is one of the areas in which our society has changed most over the past 20 years. My parents had and indeed still have an aversion to being in debt and many others of that generation are often uncomfortable with the thought of owing money. Their sons and daughters, however, have by and large a different perspective, perhaps best summed up by the phrase "live now, pay later", and they are clearly prepared to take on bigger commitments, in order to purchase today what would otherwise have had to wait until tomorrow.

This attitude change puts consumer articles within the reach of many people, provided that they are willing to borrow to facilitate payment. The vehicle most used for borrowing in the 1980s has been the credit card, and this article explores the development of both bank and retailer credit cards.

The first credit card in the United Kingdom was the Barclaycard, launched in 1966 and eventually followed in the early 1970s by Access. There are now more than 20 million bank credit cards, with Access the leader with 10 million cardholders, whilst Barclaycard

(Visa) has 8.6 million users. The comparative turnover figures also favour Access, £6.4 billion per year, as against Barclaycard's £5.4 billion. Besides the two major bank cards there are also the other bank Visa cards, for example the Co-operative Bank and the Bank of Scotland, as well as over one million of the so-called travel and entertainment cards (American Express, Diners Club).

The massive growth in bank credit cards since 1966 has been attributed to a number of factors, of which the most important is that credit card borrowing is very profitable for the sponsoring banks and as a result they have been willing to issue cards on extremely favourable terms. There are for example no joining or annual subscription fees for the major credit cards, so that the interest-free period that the cards offer between purchase and settlement of accounts is entirely without cost to the cardholder. Given the rapidly increasing level of financial sophistication of the British populace, it is no surprise that more and more people wish to hold credit cards.

In 1986 Barclaycard received 861,000 applications for new cards and they approved 590,000 of these, a record number. The 20 million bank credit cards already issued in 1986, were used for some 500 million transactions, at an average value of just under £30. The growth in both numbers of cards and their usage has been particularly spectacular since the start of the 1980s; Barclaycard for example have seen their card base grow from 6 million to the present 8.6 million and spending more than treble to £5,393 million in 1986, a figure itself 22% higher than in 1985.

Britain now uses credit cards to greater extent than any other European Community country and the credit card industry has become one of the biggest growth markets, facilitating 'payments by plastic' for millions of consumers and creating employment for many thousands of staff in the industry. The growth in usage looks set to continue as more and more retail outlets accept payment by plastic. Of particular note is the fast inroads that have been made by the major bank credit cards during 1986 into the food multiples, once fervent opponents of such payment systems.

Only Sainsbury's of the major food retailers still refuses to accept bank credit cards; the other supermarket multiples have been unable to resist customer demands to 'flash the plastic' when paying for the weekly groceries. As a result of this, Barclaycard has pushed its supermarket business up by 132% between 1985 and 1986, with sales now of £232 million and an average transaction value of £30.14.

35

Access sales rose by 172% to £217 million over the same period with an average transaction of £30.17.

These figures dispel one of the main worries of these concerned with the introduction of EFTPoS systems, that of customer resistance to cashless transactions at the checkout. However, what is disturbing for EFTPoS proponents is that cardholders are becoming increasingly sophisticated in using the free credit period offered by the card, to defer the moment when they actually have to part with the cash. The Access card for example is in their own words being increasingly used 'as a method of payment rather than simply as a means of credit'.

## Using the free credit period

Every month 40% of cardholders take advantage of the interest-free credit period before paying their accounts in full, thus incurring no interest charges. Barclaycard also have more than 40% of their customers who regularly settle in full each month, with the remainder taking on average some four months to repay the transaction. Why should those consumers who use free credit period before paying their accounts in full, relinquish that financial benefit by adopting an EFTPoS system?

The only consolation for EFTPoS backers is that as in other aspects of retailing there seems to be a 'polarisation' with regard to credit cards repayments, with some people fully aware of the interest payable on outstanding debts, whilst others seem oblivious to it. As an example of the latter attitude Debenhams in 1984 introduced for their retailer credit card a preferential rate for those willing to sign a variable direct debit to pay of the minimum amount of £5 or 5%, which ever is the larger figure, from their account. But although outstanding debts were then charged at 29.8% rather than 34.4% APR, only 12% of account holders signed up. The remaining 88% may have thought of clearing their debts monthly, but in fact only 40% of Debenhams account customers actually do this. The remainder appear to display an absence of consumer price sensitivity to credit card interest rates.

Despite the success of the bank credit cards in issuing the vast majority of the cards currently in circulation and in gaining the growth in usage represented by the example of the food multiples, the most active sector of the credit card market is that represented by retailer credit cards. These are personalised cards issued by retailers to facilitate customers paying by credit for purchases made in their own stores. By the end of 1986, it was estimated that there were some 9 million retailer credit cards in issue and that these made up the bulk of the estimated 2,000 'brands' of credit and charge cards in operation in the United Kingdom today. Again Department of Trade and Industry figures showed that of the £2,720 million of credit advanced in July 1986, Access and Visa contributed £1,110 million. The majority of the residual £1,610 million came from the rapidly expanding retailer credit cards.

The development by retailers of personalised credit cards has been and is likely to remain an area of rapid growth. Whilst there are now in total just under 30 million credit cards in circulation in the United Kingdom, this number is forecast to grow to some 50 million by the year 2000, and much of that growth will come from the issue of retailer credit cards. The outstanding example of this is the Marks & Spencer Chargecard which since its launch in April 1985 has gained well over 1.5 million cardholders and Chargecard sales now account for 12% of their United Kingdom turnover.

Marks & Spencer are undoubtedly delighted by the success of their Chargecard, particularly as their analysis shows that the average purchase on the Chargecard is £24, compared to the £22 average a cheque user spends in the store. Furthermore the most popular Chargecard buys are higher priced items like furniture and men's suits. The Chargecard should break even by the end of 1987 and by the early 1990s could contribute more than 5% of the pretax profits.

The Burton Group is currently the largest retailer credit card operator with 2.8 million accounts including those run by its Welbeck credit offshoot, which operates credit card services on behalf of a large number of other retailers. The Debenhams credit card has around 650,000 cardholders with credit sales of £166 million in 1985, a figure which represented 27% of that group's turnover. To gauge the potential that still exists for retailer credit cards we should remember that there are over 300 million credit cards in issue in the United States and that the penetration of credit sales in department stores is an average of 53% of turnover.

There are other United Kingdom retailers who are either just entering the credit card market or who are refining their offerings. Woolworths for example will be launching their own credit card in

1987 to cover their own stores as well as the Comet and B & Q chains. Storecard on the other hand is the name chosen for the amalgamation of the previous credit cards run by the Storehouse group of companies, headed by Sir Terence Conran. The new card covers Habitat, Mothercare, British Home Stores, SavaCentre and Richard shops and the Storecard holders will receive special offers on merchandise, sales previews and other customer incentives, as well as being able to use their card in BHS to draw up to £50 in cash per day, during normal shopping hours.

Why have retailers entered the credit card market so rapidly? And why does the public apparently wish to use retailer credit cards when very often a bank credit card would be just as acceptable in the retailer's outlet?

## Customer loyalty

From the retailer's point of view, a vital ingredient of successful retailing is promoting customer loyalty and this is increasingly difficult, for the boundaries between sectors are being broken down as retailers increasingly diversify through broadening their product mixes. A retailer with an own-label credit card is able to communicate directly with the customer via the monthly credit statement and in this way builds up a 'privileged customer' relationship which sustains customer loyalty.

Add to this the fact that the retailer has first hand knowledge of what exactly the customer has bought, not only in the previous month but throughout the whole length of their credit card relationship and the possibility exists of targeting special merchandise offers to customers with known buying habits.

The retailer can in addition offer a variety of financial services, banking, insurance, money management, all offered in normal retailing hours and in an atmosphere of familiarity in which many customers feel more at ease than they do in conventional banking locations. This perhaps helps to explain why some people use a retailer credit card in preference to a bank credit card. An article by the author in *Retail & Distribution Management* (September/ October 1986) further explores this issue.

Michael Bliss, Chief Executive of Fraser Financial Services, describes own-label credit cards as *the* marketing tool of the 1980s and states that retailers who integrate them into their total retail strategy can only increase profits. He stresses that the concept of the personalised credit card is very different to that of a bankers card, in that it is a much more sophisticated payment facility which improves the relationship between the retailer and its customer, as well as pre-empting a higher proportion of their spending power. No wonder then that the credit card market is so active, with both banks and retailers jostling for position and both apprehensive about the entry of other players, for example, the building societies, into the game.

At present all the major contestants are competing in an expanding market where in 1985 only 10% of all adults held a retail card while the penetration of bank issued cards stood at a rather more significant 32%. There is little doubt then that the UK credit card boom still has some way to run, indeed there is a belief that market saturation will not be reached until around 60% of adults hold a credit card and this will not occur within the next five years. Nevertheless, credit card issuers, be they retailers or bankers, are conscious that when the day comes when there is little growth left in the market itself, then the only growth will come from ensuring that the customer pulls a card from his or her wallet or purse when payment is required.

The position is best summed up by a quote from Peter Ellwood, Chief Executive of Barclaycard:

"With more and more in a finite marketplace — and we have yet to see what the building societies and some foreign banks will do in credit cards    the important thing is to offer more and more services to your members and to differentiate your card from the others".

For an example of a retailer with a clearly differentiated strategy for a credit card we need to look towards the United States. Here in 1986, the retail group Sears launched a new type of retailer credit card — the Discover card which can be used in a variety of locations outside of Sears own stores. Arrangements have been made with other service and retail establishments to accept the card and these outlets are keen to take the Discover card because the charge to those who accept it is lower than that charged by the banks and American Express etc. By November 1986, more than 450,000 other retailers accepted the Discover card, including such 'names' as K-mart, Montgomery Ward and Dayton Hudson.

As there is no initial charge to individuals for the Discover card (in contrast to the existing USA bank cards) and with the reputation of Sears behind it, the card is undoubtedly attractive and by early 1987 the Discover card base was over 8 million, with Sears predicting 10 million cardholders by the end of 1987. This makes this particular retail credit card a very serious competitor to the existing bank, travel and entertainment cards in the United States, particularly when Sears is committed to providing a wide range of financial services to its cardholders.

The Discover card gives the holder access to the Sears Family Savings Account, which provides a tiered interest rate structure on the balance of each holder's account; it gives access to the Dean Witter financial services which offer advice in loans and investments and the card can be used to obtain cash advances from automatic teller machines. This range and level of financial services has the potential to make Sears and its Discover card a major player, not just in retailing but also in the financial sector.

## The Style card

There are retailers in the United Kingdom who have perceived the potential of retailer credit cards and who are moving in the same directions as the Sears group. The Style card developed by Goldbergs of Glasgow has a number of characteristics of the Discover card, and it has the largest credit card base in Scotland, with 360,000 card holders. The article by the author in *Retail & Distribution Management* (January/February 1987) discusses the Style card, its development, and its potential in terms of financial services. United Kingdom banks have also started to realise the importance of differentiating their cards from those of their competitors. Again one of the smaller cards has been flexible enough to make the running here and the Co-operative Bank is trying to bridge the divide between a bank card and a retail credit card.

There is undoubtedly potential for retailer credit cards to move on up into the relatively untapped market for the provision of financial services. There will not be room for many retailers on this particular 'gravy train' and possibly only a retailer with the 'clout' of Sears can hope to secure the levels of consumer trust and financial muscle to succeed in emulating the Discover card and becoming a competitor to the well established bank credit cards in the United Kingdom. A retailer such as Marks & Spencer, with a rapidly expanding credit card base and a long-standing relationship of mutual trust with its customers, could well translate this into the provision of financial services.

Indeed in June 1987 Marks & Spencer acquired from Citibank Savings a further 130,000 budget card accounts. These pay interest on credit balances and Marks were able to take them over because in early 1987 they acquired licensed deposit taker status from the Bank of England. This opens up the tantalising prospect of Marks & Spencer achieving the status of a fully fledged bank. Certainly it creates the opportunity for Marks & Spencer to offer financial services to their customers through the Chargecard and to follow the Sears example of challenging the banks at their own game. We often talk of retail banking when referring to the mainstream banks; why should not a conventional retailer take on the role of the provider of financial services to its 'privileged customers'?

The Burton Group has also signalled its widening ambitions for in-store financial services by seeking Stock Exchange membership and by taking over the Money Centres currently installed in two of its Debenhams department stores. Burton's aim to open up to as many as ten new Money Centres in other Debenhams stores, with the aim of providing a wide range of financial products including shares, house and car insurance, life insurance, unit trusts, mortgages and estate agency.

The 'explosion in credit' caused in part by changing societal attitudes to debt, has set in train firstly the growth of bank credit cards and secondly the imitative rapid development of retailer credit cards. The situation in 1987 is that some retailers are well up the 'learning curve' as regards the management and marketing of credit and they are now looking to take on the banks not only in the provision of credit but also in offering other financial services to their customers. For further developments it is going to be a case of 'Watch this Space'.

# EFTPoS and Non-Cash Payment Systems

Eric Foster and Martin Houghton
*Spectra Management Support Ltd*

*There are advantages for the retailer to be gained
through the proper use of EFTPoS. In the
supermarket, payment by EFTPoS will be faster;
at the petrol stations, there should be fewer traffic
jams; in the department store, service should be
quicker. But costs for the retailer are critical.
Although some progress has been made recently,
there is still some way to go before agreement can be
reached between banks and retailers on a number
of issues, not least that of standardisation.*

T oday's consumers select from hard cash, paper money, cheques, credit cards, direct debit, instalment payment, and part exchange (barter?) — when considering how to pay for goods and services.

Developments of the technologies used in plastic cards, in computer electronics and communications make it possible for shoppers to consider a new form of payment, Electronic Funds Transfer, or EFTPoS. The principle is payment by the use of a plastic card to authorise the transfer of funds electronically — or by Direct Debit — from the shopper's bank account to that of the retailer.

This new approach to the old problem of How to Pay, or How to be Paid, brings with it many new opportunities for both retailers and their customers. EFTPoS will undoubtedly find a place alongside those other methods of payment which have evolved over the years. As a means of payment it will co-exist with cash, paper money, cheques, direct debit, and plastic money. In an evolutionary manner, over time, it may well gain considerable support because of the convenience it offers.

However, if we remember the past those enthusiasts who believe EFTPoS will give rise to a cashless society are likely to be disappointed. It seems more likely — as with its predecessors — that it will take its place alongside present methods of payment, and be used by the consumer as only one of an expanded range of options when paying for goods and services.

Retailing is not one but many businesses. When asked for the advantages for EFTPoS for the retailer, one must therefore reply "which retailer?"

In the supermarket, payment by EFTPoS will be faster, and should speed up the process of customers through the checkouts. Already some 28 per cent of payments made in UK supermarkets are non-cash, and this will grow further. Payment times using cheques are slow, and irritating for the other customers waiting in the queue.

43

At the petrol station 33 per cent of payments are non-cash, and time lost through payment with cards blocking un-usable petrol pumps must result in lost sales for the station operators.

In department stores, where purchases can be of higher value, customers are often very irritated by a long wait caused by the need to "validate" cheques with names and addresses, bankers, cards, and the often interminable search for a supervisor who has gone to tea.

Many retailers will welcome the benefits of EFTPoS — which in addition to faster and friendlier service for their customers can provide the retailer with greater security through the ability to check that the customer can pay for the merchandise before the transaction is complete.

For the retailer the costs of EFTPoS are critical. They will expect to offer this payment option to their customers at no penalty to themselves. In their view when accepting payment by EFTPoS it must not cost their businesses — or customers — more than present methods.

Over recent years the overwhelming response by ordinary people to the use of Automatic Teller Machines (ATMs), or cash dispensers, has demonstrated their willingness to support the electronic transfer of funds to and from their accounts. The growth of Direct Debit payments for settling mortgages, gas, water and other regular bills, is further evidence of this.

Payment by EFTPoS will offer the ordinary consumer an opportunity of faster payment than cheques, less queuing and will reduce the need, and risk, of carrying around large amounts of cash. Undoubtedly some consumers will find this convenience attractive and will want to take advantage of it. This could be particularly true early in a month, when they are sure of funds in their accounts, over holiday periods, during shopping sprees at pre-Christmas or sale times, when travelling long distances by car or dining out.

At other times they will undoubtedly still want to pay by cash, cheques and ordinary credit card.

On balance it is likely that consumers will welcome EFTPoS as *another* method of payment, and retailers too, *provided the charges are sensibly set,* will be the first to offer the convenience of its use in their shops.

Plastic payment and charge cards issued by the major international credit and charge card organisations, by private label card companies, or by the retailer himself, can offer the retailer an alternative to cash or cheques for the payment of goods or services. However, in order to detect fraudulent use of the cards and possible loss of revenue, a check must be made against a local floor limit, and for some transactions, the card issuer's database.

The floor limits will have been determined during negotiations between the card issuer and retailer and will be set at a level which optimises fraud risks to the costs involved in making the check at the card issuer's database.

Traditionally this check, or referral, is made through a simple telephone call to an authorisation centre specially set up by the card issuer for this purpose for all transactions exceeding the floor limit.

## The "hot card" list

When transactions are below the floor limit, they are effectively authorised by the retailer himself after consulting a paper-based "hot card" list. This is a printed list of suspect account numbers circulated regularly to retailers. However these lists are substantial and the retailer may not always take the trouble to check, particuarly during busy periods.

Some card issuers operate "charge backs" where the transaction value becomes the responsibility of the retailer if a card is accepted when it appears on the hot card list. In the case of a large store, this can amount to several thousand pounds per month.

Authorisation telephones have provided a convenient means of automating and extending existing credit card authorisation procedures.

In the UK there are now around 8000 of these installed at retail points of sale, supported by On-Line Card Services Ltd (OLCS), a company owned jointly by Access, American Express, Barclaycard and Diners Club.

For those retailers who have installed full EPoS equipment, transaction acquirers or card issuers can down-load lists of suspect card numbers to the central EPoS controller. Individual terminals then route authorisation request messages to the controller which will make an appropriate check and give a response.

Some systems have the capability to conduct authorisation and transaction data captured in real-time, but communication links and networks able to handle significant volumes of data and provide a rapid response are necessary.

EPoS/EFTPoS systems capable of supporting this type of transaction will in addition send details of the card holder's purchases to the acquirer or card issuer without the need to process paper vouchers.

For retailers who have not installed EPoS equipment, free standing EFTPoS terminals are available from several suppliers which can capture payment transaction data without the need to emboss a paper voucher. Unlike Authorisation Telephones, these enhanced data capture terminals produce a printed record of the cardholder's transaction and incorporate security features to provide protection for the data during transmission between acquirers, card issuers and retailers systems.

Once transactions are fully automated at the point-of-sale, it becomes very important to ensure that effective security is provided to protect all parties.

Security is needed to:

— Authenticate the card holder as the valid user of the card as presented, typically by the use of a PIN (Personal Identification Number), or signature. The new generation of "Smart Cards" is expected to make a valuable contribution in this area by removing the need to make a check with a remote data base to confirm the correct use of a cardholder's PIN.

— Authenticate the terminal to the transaction acquirer or card issuer, as a valid source of transaction data.

— Protect the transmission data from fraudulent alteration during transmission to acquirers or card issuers.

— Ensure that sensitive data can only be read by an authorised party.

Secure message architectures are presently in use for these applications which provide encryption based protection for the data, authentication of messages and terminals and management of the encryption "keys" used during security processing.

There is still a significant amount of work to be done in this area to agree working standards which can be supported by all the parties to a transaction. Most pilot systems presently under development are moving towards the use of international standards where these are appropriate, and the larger schemes will certainly have an influence on the shape of new standards needed for the future.

At the present time all EFTPoS schemes of significance need to use communications to a remote site for at least part of the transaction cycle.

For a retail EFTPoS installation, the communications can be logically divided as follows:
*Local Area:* The simplest means of communication from the point-of-sale uses the "dial-up" public telephone service, usually as a connection to one of the wide area networks serving the parties to the transaction. The Authorisation Telephones installed in the UK generally use this approach.

However the method, whilst widely available, is slow due to the need to support pulse dialling at 10 pps and is costed on the basis of call duration rather than the quantity of data transmitted. It is also difficult to "cluster" connections together which tends to mean multiple telephone lines, or PBX extensions. This introduces significant additional installation costs for the retailer.

In the UK British Telecom have introduced a range of local area connection services under the name of "Cardway" aimed specifically at retail payment transactions. This service provides a direct link from the point-of-sale to the local BT exchange, from where it interconnects with the public data network PSS.

## Local Area Networks

An in-store LAN (Local Area Network) can also be very effective in concentrating messages from the point-of-sale to a store controller, from where a single connection to a wide area network can be made. This local in-store network will provide the vehicle for both EFT and EPoS messages and forms part of the retailers management information system.

*Wide Area:* As the name implies, wide area communications are used to link remote parties to each other. The network can be built up from the use of high capacity leased lines, or by using switching techniques to optimise the use of the network.

Packet switching techniques, where the message is automatically divided up into discrete "packets" of information prior to transmission across the network, have become the most likely source of present generation wide-area network for EFTPoS.

A national EFTPoS scheme is considered by the UK banking community to be a major shift in the banking payment structure of the nation, and its development covers strategic issues such as individual market share, competition and the extent of co-operation between parties.

There have been many attempts during the last 10 years to introduce a single, integrated EFTPoS scheme for the UK. Criticism of these proposals has been directed at the size and inflexibility of a centralised and closed system which has been unable to embrace the developments of the participating parties.

Initial plans were almost entirely driven by the clearing banks with little regard for the impact on other services such as credit and in-store cards, and on retailer's private networks.

National EFTPoS is seen as a new retail payment delivery system as significant in its development as the introduction of automated cheque clearing and credit cards, and is expected to affect all parts of the economic structure, including retailing, banking, building societies and many other financial institutions.

The Bank of England in its regulatory capacity has expressed the view that a smoothly functioning payment system can best be achieved through a co-operative and orderly approach to the development of suitable standards for the key areas of security, system reliability, network management and control, message structures and terminal specifications.

One of the problems is to find a balance between the burden of development costs and the benefits to be obtained in what is seen as a competitive area where technology will allow the entry of many new value added service providers.

In practice there has been an evolutionary influence in the development of a national EFTPoS scheme. The major credit and charge card organisations have shown the way forward through the agreement on join specifications for Authorisation Telephones and the new generation of Payment Terminals as used by Access, American Express and Barclaycard for voucherless data capture at the point-of-sale. These terminals can accept the cards of any organisation adopting the jointly supported standard known as IBRO Standard 40.

This standard covers such matters as message formats, security communications and installation and replacement of terminals. Although in its present form it is unlikely to be suitable for a truly national EFTPoS scheme involving many service providers, it could be developed further as the basis of a new standard.

A number of standards from the International Standards Organisation already in existence or draft form, are likely to be adopted for national EFTPoS in the interests of maintaining multi-vendor supply arrangements.

The current development scheme will see the introduction of a small inaugural service involving 2000 terminals in three UK locations during 1988, (Southampton, Leeds and Edinburgh) and is intended to set the standards to be followed in a national system. This initial service will be centrally controlled by EFTPoS UK Ltd, the company set up within the structure, membership rules and framework of APACS (the Association for Payment Clearing Services), to develop national EFTPoS.

## A compatible system

Members will have the option to continue within a joint development programme or to establish a "devolved" but compatible system as transaction acquirers establishing their own retailer relationships and terminal networks, all within regulations for the national scheme.

EFTPoS UK Ltd will offer a complete service to retailers and are at present working hard to establish a clear identity as the provider of a faster, easier and better way to pay. The Inaugural Service is intended to test the various business relationships and technologies proposed for national EFTPoS, and if successful will allow members, either collectively or as value added service providers, to support an open and competitive system.

A truly integrated national EFTPoS system will be a unique and complex undertaking and will need to address the following:

— Terminal standards which will allow secure operation in a number of different retail environments and will make it possible for retailers to incorporate EFTPoS into their own PS equipment when they wish to do so. Retailers will be free to choose equipment from their preferred suppliers, who themselves will be free to consider whether to make products available which conform to published EFTPoS UK standards.

— The development of a high capacity managed network allowing widespread local access to terminals.

— The development of a transaction message switching system with very high availability, together with methods for settlement and reconciliation between members.

The proposals for national EFTPoS will allow retailers to accept a wide range of card based services, including In-Store Cards, Credit

Cards and Travel and Entertainment Cards, in addition to the new Unified Debit Cards.

The building societies have a significant advantage over most clearing banks in the EFTPoS debate, in that they have on-line transaction processing systems more suited to the demands made by EFTPoS for real-time transaction management.

The larger societies such as the Abbey National and Nationwide have established linked on-line networks of ATM machines through joint ventures with the Co-operative Bank and National Giro Bank. The LINK and FTS networks provide mechanisms for the acceptance of member institutes' cards at all terminal outlets.

This helps the societies overcome the disadvantage they have by being regionally based. Each society card holder base tends to be localised within the "home" region, but networking has liberated member societies and allowed the expansion of their services without the need to open a large national network of branches.

Now that societies are free to offer a growing range of services, using their electronic transaction management capability, there have been examples of EFTPoS experiments such as the Anglia's Northampton-based service, now to be shared with Barclaycard. Because of their traditional background as savings and mortgage institutions, societies will need to build business relationships with retailers who should see a new and growing breed of customer with direct access to "savings" accounts.

With their traditional "thrift" image, it is interesting to consider the effect of their entry into EFTPoS on cardholders who dislike the notion of "credit" in the use of plastic payment cards.

Due to the very nature of the subject, EFTPoS terminals in use at present have in general tended to be free-standing devices specially developed for the support of non-cash payments at the point of sale.

The reason for this is not hard to recognise when the following points are examined:

— EFTPoS usually means links to several institutions.

— Terminals need to be of modest cost since additional terminals will be used by the retailer at the POS for providing retail management information.

— There is a clear need for standards for messages, communications, security and user interfaces.

It is not practical within the cost constraints imposed on the terminals, to support several different standards for these key functions. Therefore a single standard is preferred which will allow an EFTPoS terminal to establish a session with any one of several card issuing, or transaction acquiring institutions. Such standards are by definition complex and take time to agree, particularly if they are to apply to international users and be ratified by standards bodies such as ISO or BSI.

During the development phases for these standards, whether they be through EFTPoS UK Ltd or by practical experimentation and acceptance, changes will be necessary to the terminals and other system components. It is far better to confine such changes to small free standing devices than to fully integrated EFTPoS terminals.

The long term view of retail electronic payments would include the support of non-cast secure financial data capture and full EFTPoS defined as:

$$EFTPoS = (authorisation) + (Secure data capture)$$
$$+ (settlement \& reconciliation)$$

However to achieve full integration of EFT and POS functions, manufacturers must see a stable, standardised set of conditions on which to base the considerable investments needed for product development.

## Familiar presentation

Users of terminals, that is card holders using their cards to purchase goods or services, will expect a familiar presentation of the procedures at EFTPoS terminals. This does not mean that all terminals will be exactly the same, but it does mean that key functions are presented to the user in a similar way to encourage use of the services.

There are at present many "pilot" EFTPoS and voucherless transaction data capture schemes distributed over different sections of the retail scene.

With certain exceptions, the stated objectives of these experiments are to test the varying types of technology used and to develop working relationships with retail partners.

The experience gained will prove invaluable in the production of suitable standards and working practices to allow for the merging of compatible schemes where common business benefits would result.

# Trends in food retailing

Dr John A. Beaumont
*Chief Executive, Institute of Grocery Distribution*

*The move towards size is one of the factors which has characterised food retailing outlets in the past few years, the superstore being the obvious example. In the '70s this space tended to be filled with non-food; now there's no doubt that the major grocers are returning to selling what they're best at —food. Fresh foods are particularly in demand, and health foods are no longer a minority fad.*

In such a mature market as food it might well be assumed that its production and distribution would be a relatively stable commercial activity, subject only to marginal changes. Against a static population, a cursory glance at national economic data does indeed confirm a total food market demonstrating little real growth. Any suggestion of an unchanging market must, however, end at that point. Indeed, with the exception of that tendency to demonstrate sluggish overall volume, the market has shown a marked propensity to develop and diversify. Furthermore it may be argued that a major part of the fundamental changes which have emerged may be traced to developments initiated by food retailers, motivated by increasingly competitive forces to identify and meet even the smallest consumer change.

It is common knowledge that over the past two decades an increasingly wealthy population has undergone widespread demographic and social change. A broader education, whether derived from formal learning, television or overseas travel has led to significant changes in habits and attitudes. The food market has been deeply influenced by such changes. Geographic changes in population location, from the North to the South, from urban to suburban areas has required the re-siting of retail outlets. The working patterns of women and the greater emphasis placed on leisure time have put a considerable premium on the provision of convenience in food products. A more sophisticated outlook has introduced a new flexibility in buying patterns, encouraging greater emphasis on variety, product initiative and quality of presentation.

Response to such a changing consumer demand has been widespread throughout the food industry. A more exotic national palate has opened up the market for a much wider range of domestic and overseas items, from ethnic speciality foods to a more extensive range of fresh produce lines. The demand for variety and convenience has stimulated increasing efforts from the manufacturing industry to provide a widening range of processed goods. Growth in consumer

53

durables such as freezers and microwave ovens have had an immense impact on the provision of appropriate food products. In recent years an increasing awareness of dietary factors amongst consumers has seen a growing emphasis on fresh foods and has led to a major reassessment of the use of additives in food formulation.

If we are seeking to identify those changes which have been *most* fundamental within the nature of food retailing in recent years then we must pay particular attention to the changing role and influence which this sector has had on the food market in general. For much of the past forty years retailing has played a somewhat passive role in determining the way in which consumer demand has been met, with the central marketing control and management being with the supplier. Consumer research and advertising, product development and overseas sourcing have largely been outside the scope of the retail trade.

### Growing competition

The last few years, however, have seen an awakening of activity in these areas by the retailer, particularly the grocery retailer. Driven by growing competitive forces to find ways to differentiate their offerings, the major companies have increasingly sought to take over a central marketing role. It is indeed this factor which has been at the heart of the changing face of British food retailing.

A common theme running through most parts of the retail trade in the past few years has been the growing importance of the large multiple organisation. Such businesses across retailing have been accounting for an increasing proportion of available sales. A major factor in this growth may be traced to their relative success in recognising and adapting to consumer change, while the subsequent size of their business has given them easier access to capital for expansion, and enabled them to accumulate the necessary expertise and system technology to progress. Economies of scale in buying must also be seen as providing significant price advantage.

Within food retailing these trends have been most obvious among the traditional grocery operators. Arguably the growth ambitions of a relatively small number of such companies have led to comprehensive change throughout the entire retail food market. Certainly they have led to the grocers' achieving a predominant role in food marketing and a consequent change in the structure of the supply

54

and wholesale sectors. Equally their growth, and the pressure which this has put on the rest of the industry, has provided considerable impetus for change and the search for commercial and technological improvement.

At the heart of such changes has undoubtedly been the juxtaposition of corporate growth and the relatively static nature of their core food markets. While growing in current price terms, household food spending has shown little real increase. Official figures suggest for example a growth of only 5 per cent in food spending in the fifteen years to 1986 compared with an overall rise in consumer spending of some 32 per cent with areas like consumer durables achieving increases in excess of 80 per cent. Against such a background firms like J Sainsbury and Tesco have grown from around £200 million to nearly £4000 million annual sales.

An examination of such figures clearly invites the question, how could such corporate sales growth be achieved? Indeed it is in examining this question which leads to an explanation of some of the key trends which have occurred.

As a first stage of analysis one can identify three main pathways for the growth of the major grocery multiples. These may be stated as follows:

a)  A movement into product ranges outside those traditionally sold by the grocer.
b)  A deviation of trade from other types of operator, namely the Co-operative Societies and the Independents.
c)  Corporate growth through acquisition and merger.

## Diversification

The first of these options, which may be regarded as diversification, has been used extensively and has led to a considerable widening of the range of goods available within the typical grocery outlet. Foremost in this area has been a move into food lines traditionally handled by specialists such as carcase meat, fresh produce and bakery products. While spearheaded by the multiples such range extension has been common among all types of grocer, to the extent that this sector now accounts for a significant proportion of total sales in these areas, with a consequent decline in the role of the specialist food retailers.

Increasingly in recent years the inclusion of fresh foods in the product mix of new grocery outlets has been a common feature. While offering scope for growth they have also proved attractive in having relatively high margins and in providing scope to differentiate those retailers who could demonstrate superior quality and freshness.

Diversification by grocers into non-food lines has also been a common feature, but progress has been mixed, and the policy adopted by different operators has varied considerably. In the early 1970s much experimentation took place into the stocking of such lines as durable goods and clothing. Subsequent growth of competition in some of these areas, however, has since limited their uptake within the grocery trade, and the emphasis in diversification has been towards fresh foods. It is still true to say, however, that (particularly in the larger stores) non-foods are sold, but this is mainly limited to the smaller household wares, leisure goods and clothing.

## Decline in Co-ops

For the multiples as a group a considerable part of their growth has been achieved by taking an increasing proportion of the total sales of the grocery sector, with a consequent decline in the relative importance of the Co-operative Societies and Independents (see Table 1).

### Table 1. Grocery Market Shares by Type of Operator

|  | 1970 | 1980 | 1985 |
|---|---|---|---|
| Multiples | 42.0 | 60.9 | 70.1 |
| Co-operatives | 15.0 | 14.2 | 11.6 |
| Independents | 43.0 | 24.9 | 18.3 |

*Source:* A. C. Nielsen.

Among the multiple and co-operative sectors the growth of many of the larger organisations has been enhanced by mergers and acquisitions. Within the Co-operative Movement there has been a progressive programme of amalgamations which has reduced the

56

number of individual societies from 357 in 1970 to 95 in 1986. Such movement has largely occurred by mutual arrangement and has allowed a considerable rationalisation in store operations, marketing policies and distribution systems.

Similarly there has been a great deal of rationalisation within the multiple sector, but much of this has come about as a result of corporate acquisition. Over the past ten years very many well known companies have been taken over by competitors and their names and operations absorbed. As a result of such acquisitions there has been a major concentration within the multiple sector. Currently some five companies account for over 73 per cent of the multiple sector or 52 per cent of the grocery retail trade as a whole. But it must be pointed out that the two leading multiples, Sainsbury and Tesco, have developed through internal growth and not through acquisition.

An increase in the average size for each sector reflects the tendency since the mid-1970s to build larger units. For the multiples, for example, an average of 14,600 sq ft was recorded in 1976 compared with a figure of around 20,000 sq ft in the years since then.

An explanation for the move to larger stores lies in two main areas. The first revolves around the question of economies of scale. Operating costs per square foot, notably capital and labour, decline generally with increasing size and thus give advantage when competitive conditions favour low cost operation. Concurrently an increase in size provides greatly increased scope for range extension which has been such a feature of more recently favoured trading formats. Additionally the operation of a smaller number of larger units reduces the overall management problems associated with controlling the very large modern retail business. In particular it simplifies the distribution configuration within such organisations.

## Large superstores

While there has been a general trend to larger store operation there has latterly been some indication of stratification of store size according to store operation and chosen trading format.

At the upper end of size scale there has been a significant move into superstores having a sales area in excess of 25,000 sq ft. Starting around 1970, the superstore building programme has developed with the current total number of such units standing at 457. Emerging first in the North of England such units have been developed throughout the country, although the availability of sites and planning difficulties has meant their density in Southern England remains relatively low.

With an average selling area of around 38,250 sq ft these stores allow adequate treatment of a full food range as well as a range of non-food lines. While not exclusively so, these stores have tended to be placed in areas outside the traditional High Street, where larger sites allowing adequate single level car parking are available.

The distribution of superstores by operator suggest that those companies primarily concerned are Tesco, Asda, J Sainsbury, Morrisons and the Dee Corporation; with Co-operative Societies also major operators (see Table 2).

### Table 2. Superstores by Major Operators 1987

| | |
|---|---:|
| Argyll | 14 |
| Asda | 92 |
| Dee | 75 |
| Wm. Low | 3 |
| Wm. Morrison | 24 |
| J Sainsbury* | 56 |
| G. T. Smith | 1 |
| Tesco† | 124 |
| Co-ops | 62 |
| Independents | 5 |
| | 457 |

*Including SavaCentre.    †Including Hillards.

*Source:* IGD Research Services.

While superstores may represent the more spectacular face of grocery store development there has been a consistent building programme in the size category 10-25,000 sq ft. Indeed in numbers terms their development has been in the majority in recent years. Edge-of-town sites have been used for a proportion of such stores but perhaps not surprisingly there has been a majority of activity in re-developed Town Centre locations. Such stores have tended to concentrate on providing an extended food range, with much less emphasis on non-foods. Operations making up the majority within this size category have been Argyll, Gateway, Waitrose and Safeway.

**Leaving out food**

The large mixed retailers have tended to drop foods from their range, witness the withdrawal by Woolworths and British Home Stores in the past few years. Only Marks & Spencer can be quoted as making a spectacular success of their food operation. With sales now approaching £1,500 million in food they have remained at the forefront of development. Concentrating largely on fresh and chilled foods they have been active in expanding the niche for high quality convenience products. Until recently such food sales were incorporated with existing mixed store units, but currently experiments are being conducted into specialist food stores.

The onset of increasingly competitive trading conditions and the growth of very large businesses at the centre of the grocery retail trade has seen the adoption of much more professional management and the development of more formalised systems. New technology has clearly played an important part but this has been complemented by a move to adopt more appropriate management and operating structures.

**Product coding**

As early as 1972 steps were taken to introduce unique product coding and scanning into the UK grocery trade, which began the trend towards a more refined knowledge of product sales and handling. Following the initial enthusiasm for such moves there has been a relatively protracted development phase while firms realised that such a powerful data capture facility required a complete re-appraisal of their whole management information control procedure before full economic benefits would be achieved. Only recently have the leading companies been in a position to re-base their whole business operation on a more sophisticated technology. As a result we can now expect to see the emergence of full scanning utilisation among the major retailers during the next five years.

As part of this trend to a more quantitative approach to retailing there have been major developments in product range determination and space planning. The onset of the larger store and the level of capital expenditure required, have sharpened the need to assess more effectively the real costs and profitability of space use. Such techniques as Direct Product Profitability, first mooted some 30 years ago in the United States of America, are returning to isolate with far more precision the contribution being made to overall store profitability by individual product lines. Coupled with more objective space planning models such methods will offer a much more concise means of managing the retail food business.

At the very centre of the changes in the nature of retail food operation has been the tendency for the main food companies to alter their perception of their role in the whole marketing process. This can be clearly traced from the onset of the current phase in trading conditions starting in the early 1970s.

It was at this time, associated with economic recession and the worst effects of inflation, that concentration in the trade began to gather speed and new trading formats began to emerge. Underpinned by significant increases in real labour cost in the early 1970s, emphasis moved rapidly towards seeking lower cost operation and lower prices as a means of chasing increased volume. It was at this stage that the average size of store openings almost doubled and limited range discounting emerged. At this stage, when such new techniques were confined to only a few operators, the relative cost and thus price advantage, could be played by such firms as a primary promotional ploy. This period saw a major increase in retail advertising, based primarily around the relative benefits of price. The majority of advertisements were dominated by consideration of low prices.

As the new techniques and technology became more widely adopted the spread of operational efficiency across the industry narrowed and so too the efficacy of majoring on price as a promotional tool declined. This happily coincided with a reduction in the level of inflation and consumer pre-occupation with price as the major motivating factor in purchasing decisions.

### Creating an identity

This stage in the evolution of grocery retailing strategy, around 1980, saw a search for new avenues to create competitive advantage. The matter was made more urgent by the pressure from increasing concentration to differentiate the various retail offerings; that is to create a retail brand identity. A major part of the solution was found in a move to include fresh foods, a domain previously dominated by the specialist retailers.

Competition had succeeded in lowering margins on traditional grocery products, and fresh foods had thus an additional advantage in offering rather more substantial gross profits. Concurrently the trend to larger stores provided the scope to allow more space to include such ranges and furthermore to do the job more effectively, with greater emphasis on service. Fruit and vegetables, carcass meat, fresh fish, delicatessen and in-store bakeries were beginning to have a profound impact on the average grocery store environment.

As the years have progressed these underlying needs have intensified and the treatment of fresh foods has received greater emphasis and attention. At the same time the emphasis given to these product ranges in promotional campaigns has gained greater attention. More recently trends in consumer awareness of dietary considerations has created an additional stimulus to the benefits of "fresh" food which in turn has added weight to the retailers' determination to retain this as a central plank to their promotional programme.

## Marketing role

The increasing emphasis on quality and the need to differentiate particular retailing images has permeated the entire business operation of most major grocers. This has further emphasised the determination of the companies to take on a central role in the marketing operations even in the traditional dry grocery areas previously dominated by the manufacturers. Central to this has been the growth of the retailers own brands. In almost every case there has been an increase in the emphasis placed on such activity. Figures summarising the global move to own labels are demonstrated in Table 3.

Own label has for many years been associated with Marks & Spencer and J Sainsbury, but recent years have seen growing emphasis by others such as Tesco, Safeway, Argyll and Gateway. Even Asda, traditionally dominated by manufacturers' brands has introduced an extensive own label range in the past year or so.

The latest manifestation of the impact of retailers' influence on the food market has been in their recent moves into range extension.

Following on their moves to extend into fresh food product groups they have now put considerable effort into extending the range of items within such categories, as well as in traditional grocery product groups. The number of lines incorporated into a typical store (which has in itself grown in size) has increased considerably and in some cases has almost doubled in a decade. Such a trend is fully compatible with the underlying attempts to move fully to meet a widening consumer taste and to underline the retail image of extended range and a high quality of food retail service.

---

**Table 3. Own Label Share of Multiple Packaged Grocery Turnover 1978-85**

| Year | % Own Label in Multiples |
|---|---|
| 1978 | 23.0 |
| 1979 | 22.2 |
| 1980 | 21.9 |
| 1981 | 22.9 |
| 1982 | 24.8 |
| 1983 | 26.9 |
| 1984 | 29.0 |
| 1985 | 30.0 |

*Source:* AGB/TCA/Nielsen/Euromonitor.

---

**Phases in the Evolution of Competitive Advantage**

| 1970s | 1980s | 1990s |
|---|---|---|
| Price | Price | Price |
| | Fresh foods | Fresh foods |
| | Quality | Quality |
| | | Range |
| | | Service |

---

Perhaps of more fundamental long-term importance to the domestic food market has been an emerging awareness by retailers of the international possibilities of product sourcing. Many retailers are now seeking the support of overseas producers to back up their attempts to provide the consumer with a broader range of products. Increasingly the range of foods available within the typical grocery store is being supplemented by speciality foods from overseas.

# Out of Town Exodus

Russell Schiller
*Head of Research, Hillier Parker*

*Since 1984 out of town shopping has made a leap forward; the number of out of town regional shopping centres proposed of over 500,000 sq ft rose from one in early 1984 to some 40 by the end of 1986. Local authority planners are worried, but unsure of their ground; our "weak and confused" planning response is rather different from that of most of our continental neighbours who have achieved a more consistent policy.*

The middle years of the 1980s have seen a crucial change in the locational pattern of British retailing. What has happened is that the town centre has lost its monopoly of comparison shopping. This loss of monopoly does not necessarily mean the beginning of the end of retailing in the town centre. It means, rather, that there will be a variety of retail formats of which the town centre will be only one.

The movement of retailing away from town centres can be traced as far back as the Gem stores of the mid-1960s. From that modest and none too successful beginning, decentralisation has steadily grown. It can be seen as three waves, with the first involving food, the second bulky goods, and the third comparison shopping.

Superstore groups, like Asda, expanded off-centre food retailing through the 1970s. It is interesting to recall that the early superstores often gave over half their floor space to non-food goods. The hope was that food would attract shoppers who would then buy high margin durable goods. This effort largely failed, with Woolco being probably the most well known example, and superstores today place a far stronger emphasis on food. It was widely felt at that time that the town centre was secure in its monopoly of comparison shopping, and as a result the mid-1970s saw record amounts of town centre shopping schemes being opened.

The second wave of decentralisation began in the mid-70s and involved bulky goods such as DIY and furniture, and branded goods such as white electricals and cars. Garden centres have also expanded rapidly.

It is interesting that the planners gave less opposition to the second wave of decentralisation than they did to the first. One reason was the term stores, which is a confusing contradiction in terms. It is, however, a good description of the first stores which occupied redundant industrial buildings. A second reason was that many retail warehouses sold goods like timber and sanitary ware which had never previously been sold in the town centre.

The second wave did compete with the town centre in fields such as hardware, furniture and electrical goods, but it was rightly felt that the town centre could not supply the large floorspace and adjacent surface level car parking being demanded by the retailers. So long as clothing and similar small, high value comparison goods remained, the town centre's monopoly looked secure.

The third wave of decentralisation involves clothing and other comparison goods. It has arrived more rapidly than the first two waves, indeed one can date it almost to the day/ In May 1984 Marks & Spencer announced its intention to open out-of-town stores. This decision and, to a lesser extent, the government's willingness to allow retailing in Enterprise Zones, provided a catalyst for durable decentralisation.

This is illustrated very vividly by the level of new development. Total shopping centre floorspace in the pipeline remained constant at around 30m sq ft between 1980 and 1984. By the end of 1986 it had risen to 100m sq ft. The number of out-of-town regional shopping centres proposed of over 500,000 sq ft rose from one in early 1984 to some 40 by the end of 1986.

Probably the most important change was in the attitude of the national multiple groups. Prior to 1984, many had noticed the second wave movement out-of-town and had responded by hedging their bets. They launched their own retail warehouse operations in parallel to their main High Street chain. Thus W H Smith started Do It All and Woolworths bought B&Q and Comet. After 1984 they began to look out-of-town for their comparison goods operation. Thus Boots launched Children's World and John Lewis Partnership announced plans for a free standing non-fashion department store near High Wycombe.

John Hall, developer of the Metro Centre in the Gateshead Enterprise Zone, has said that following Marks & Spencer's decision to locate in his Centre, town centres will never be the same again. Nicolas Ridley, Secretary of State for the Environment, said of the out-of-town movement (*The Times*, 17th January, 1987): "It is a bigger force than I. It is a mistake to say that I must stop it or that it can be stopped. Examples from all over the world show that it can't. It can be accelerated by traffic congestion. It can be slowed down by improving traffic flow, but I don't think it can be stopped with the powers that government has". The evidence certainly suggests a momentum towards comparison decentralisation which will be hard to stop.

Although the change during 1984-87 is fundamental, it does not imply the ending of mainstream comparison retailing in town centres. The durable multiples which are currently planning to go out-of-town aim to keep their existing assets in the town centre. This is the greatest guarantee of the continuing health of comparison shopping in its traditional home. Marks & Spencer sees its out-of-town operation as an extension to its 265 town centre stores rather than as an alternative. The Company emphasise that it is expanding its town centre operation at a faster rate than it is investing out-of-town.

The sheer complexity of development in Britain will slow the pace of out-of-town development so that the year 2000 will see the household names with a large majority of their stores still in the town centres. What has changed is that there is now a choice of location. The town centre has lost its monopoly in the place it probably matters most: the minds of the national multiple retailers.

## Accessibility and land cost

There are strong underlying pressures in favour of out-of-town retailing. These apply both to comparison as well as convenience shopping, and they apply evenly to the shopper, the retailer and the developer. They can be grouped into two basic causes: accessibility and land cost.

The majority of shoppers have access to a car and find it convenient to use it for shopping where possible. The goods which the retailer sells arrive in his shop by lorry. Both shopper and retailer, therefore, find advantages in locations offering easy access and convenient parking. The traditional town centre cannot compete in this respect. This message emerged clearly as long ago as 1963 when Buchanan produced his report, 'Traffic in Towns' for the Minister of Transport. With public transport, town centres provided the location most accessible to the surrounding area. Now for the motorist they are among the least accessible locations.

Congestion is a very powerful enemy of town centre retailing. The one consolation is that congestion can also apply out-of-town. As the decentralisation of population and employment continues, the relative difference in accessibility between town centre and out-of-town decreases. Several great American cities, notably Washington

DC, are experiencing suburban traffic congestion around out-of-town shopping and campus offices sites. We can see something of the same phenomenon in the Home Counties where the country lanes of Berkshire and Hertfordshire are already experiencing rush hour traffic jams. Accessibility is, nevertheless, a powerful force working towards the loosening of our present urban structure.

The second basic reason for decentralisation is the differential in land costs. Cost in general tends to be substantially lower in fringe locations than in town centres. Development is simpler and quicker, construction is less complicated and retail operations are more efficient. Many of these cost advantages are a by-product of accessibility, but the cost of land is also important.

As Tesco has pointed out, the cost in land for a supermarket is markedly higher in the town centre than out-of-town. As with accessibility, there are signs that the differential is narrowing with superstores paying occasionally up to £2m per acre for a favourable out-of-town site, but it is likely to stay significant.

Out-of-town development can be divided between planned centres and the remainder. The retailers themselves often straddled both types of development. Supermarket and retail warehouse operators for example are fairly indifferent whether they locate within a centre or not. An examination of their sites-wanted advertisements shows great emphasis on catchment population, good main road frontage, good parking, and adequately sized flat sites. There is rarely a mention of the need to be near other retailers.

In practice they often locate near each other on radial roads or by-passes and concede that these American style retail strips create a type of retailing ambience which works to their benefit. This applies also to the comparison third wave retailers such as Toys R Us, World of Leather and Boots' Children's World. Toys R Us have a store opposite Brent Cross on the other side of the North Circular Road, and Children's World have opened in Cricklewood. Both locations could be described as free standing, but both benefit from other retailing nearby.

It is significant that some durable multiples in Britain, such as Marks & Spencer, are prepared to consider free standing sites whereas similar operations in America would be reluctant to locate outside a planned centre. Partly this may be due to a lack of sites suitable for planned centres and partly to the feeling that a free standing location will be less damaging to the town centre.

Marks & Spencer's second out-of-town store, on the A10 near Cheshunt, is located next to an existing Tesco with a few unit shops. A store in America with similar power in the clothing market would prefer to anchor a planned centre. In this respect Britain appears to be adopting a novel out-of-town format.

Out-of-town retail development which takes the form of planned centres can be divided into four types. The smallest of these are the speciality centres. These consist mainly of small independent units selling quality merchandise of interest to tourists and visitors. Examples are Albert Dock, Liverpool, the Canutes Pavilion Centre in the Southampton Docks and Covent Garden.

Most of these centres offer under 100,000 sq ft of retailing and would more accurately be described as off-centre rather than out-of-town. They require a location which attracts visitors such as a waterfront position or a converted historic building. A museum or similar tourist attraction nearby is also desirable.

## The district centre

The second out-of-town format is the district centre. In size this usually runs between 100,000 and 300,000 sq ft and is anchored by a superstore. The district centre is a familiar form both in Britain and abroad. Examples are Hempstead Valley, Cameron Toll, West Swindon and Beaumont Leys. These centres offer a fairly even mix of food and routine durable goods and provide a modern format for the traditional centre catering for the family weekly shop.

Retail parks began in the early 1980s as groups of retail warehouses on industrial estates. Early examples such as the Aireside Centre, Leeds, and Poole Commerce Centre, resemble industrial estates in their layout. In most early retail parks each retail warehouse is free standing with its own car park and little emphasis on walkways between the stores.

The trend is for retail parks to improve in design and come more to resemble actual parks. More emphasis is being placed on landscaping and there is a preference for grouping in a terraced format.

They are, in fact, coming more to resemble conventional shopping centres, with better facilities for shoppers, such as covered walkways and seating areas, or even cafés.

The equivalent of the retail park in America is the strip centre which consists of a group of stores parallel to a main road with, say, a

69

home improvement store (DIY) anchoring one end, a discount furniture store the other, and conventional smaller shops in between. The retail park differs from this because it still shows signs of its industrial origins. Unit shops are missing partly because there is the felling among planners that the inclusion of unit shops would make the retail park more competitive with the town centre. This idea is mistaken since the type of traders which would occupy such units would tend to be services or convenience retailers.

The fourth and most spectacular form of out-of-town shopping centre is the regional centre. This consists of 500,000 sq ft or more of comparison retailing. The best example in Britain is Brent Cross, which opened in 1976. Milton Keynes can lay claim to being the second, and the Metro Centre in Gateshead the third. The regional shopping centre is well known in America and other parts of the world. It typically contains two department stores and a number of specialist clothing and footwear shops. Just as the district centre is the modern form of the smaller town centre or suburban centre, so the regional centre is the modern form of the higher order city centre.

The success of John Hall in attracting Marks & Spencer to the Metro Centre turned what had been a retail park into a regional centre. Experience has shown that as retail parks increase in size they reach a ceiling at around 3-400,000 sq ft. Expansion above that in practice means bringing in the fashion and footwear retailers and the format changes from the retail park to the covered mall. This radical change of format occurred in Metro Centre and less dramatically in the Merry Hill Centre near Dudley.

There was an abnormal number of proposals for regional centres during 1986. The number of new proposals during 1987 has been lower, and some of those proposed earlier have been withdrawn. The problem which the developer of a regional centre faces above all is to find a suitable site which is acceptable to both planners and retailers. Preferred locations, such as motorway intersections, have a tendency in Britain to be classified as Green Belt and be placed out-of-bounds for shopping. What is available is redundant industrial land, most of it in locations unsuited for shopping use.

By taking a relaxed view on the question of impact on town centres, the Government has allowed proposals for regional centres and other forms of decentralised shopping to go ahead. It has not, however, seen to the provision of suitable sites. It has allowed the ends but not the means. The result is that retailing, that most location sensitive of all activities, is being forced to adopt out-of-town locations which would not even be short listed by shopping centre developers in most other countries.

There are two abnormalities to out-of-town retailing in Britain. The first is the retail park, which is a format unknown elsewhere in the world, and the second is the tendency of comparison retailers to locate in free standing or near free standing locations. Both to a large extent result from the willingness of Government, both local and national, to use the pressure for out-of-town retail development as a means of bringing redundant industrial land into use.

Out of-town retailing runs against the whole ethos of British planning. The out-of-town superstores of the 1970s were often opposed as much because they went against the adopted plan as because of impact on the town centre. That battle was lost and "retail warehouse" met less opposition.

Now that town centres are being directly threatened by the decentralisation of comparison retailing many local authority planners are seriously worried, but feel unsure of their ground.

## Job creation

In 1986 and 1987 a number of regional centres were given planning consent with little difficulty. In the northern half of the country the argument about job creation carried considerable weight. The precise level of impact was felt to be uncertain, as was the attitude of central government should a refusal by the local planning authority be taken to appeal.

The somewhat weak and confused planning response to the third wave of decentralisation is a far cry from the confident days of the post-war years. It is also a far cry from the experience of most of our continental neighbours who have managed to achieve a more consistent policy on the ground without as rich a town planning tradition as Britain enjoys.

In most continental towns comparison retailing appears firmly anchored in the town centre. Round the periphery are hypermarkets, furniture stores and similar fast growing types of retailing. Town centres generally have experienced less redevelopment and expansion than in Britain, and less effort has been made to accommodate the car. Continental cities often contain the concentration of quality specialist shopping in an attractive environment which many

71

commentators see as the future of the larger British town centres.

The attitude to out-of-town retailing in many European countries has been a mirror image of British policy. The early phase was tolerated on the continent and opposed in Britain. Now out-of-town is being restricted there whilst the British attitude has become more tolerant.

The original British planning strategy of clustering retailing into town and suburban centres has proved unworkable and has been steadily abandoned. Ironically it is the continentals who have proved more pragmatic. They permitted out-of-town development when hypermarkets first arrived and were seen to be too big to be accommodated in the town centre, and have since imposed limits when the impact threatened to undermine town centre retailing.

The *laissez-faire* attitude of our Government has led to competition between out-of-town developers, something which is commonplace in America but new to Britain. As a result it is the retailers, particularly Marks & Spencer, which are choosing between rival regional centres. Marks & Spencer's decision to take a store in the Meadowhall scheme near Sheffield effectively meant the end of the proposed Parkgate regional centre at Rotherham nearby. The board of Marks & Spencer in Baker Street thus made as important a contribution to retail planning in South Yorkshire as did local or central government. We could see more "Baker Street planning" in future.

Despite the huge increase in proposals for regional centres in 1986, the number opening in the next few years is likely to be much more limited. A total of some dozen in the next few years seems a reasonable forecast. This number in itself should not cause the destruction of town centre retailing in the way that has occurred in America.

Regional centres, however, are far from being the only out-of-town developments which could take durable sales from town centres. It is the comparison stores in free standing locations or small centres which are likely in the long run to have a greater impact. Free standing locations are smaller, easier to find, and have a smaller impact than large out-of-town centres. There could therefore be more out-of-town comparison retailers outside rather than inside regional shopping centres, and they are likely to affect a wider range of town centres.

The town centre must improve its environmental quality to meet the out-of-town competition. Probably the most effective single way of doing this is to increase the amount of pedestrianisation. Britain is far behind the continent, particularly Germany, in pedestrianisation. Once traffic is removed it is immediately possible to improve amenities and to provide street theatre.

Town centres are losing their monopoly of comparison retailing, and the momentum towards decentralisation is sufficiently strong that it would be difficult to stop it. British town centres are likely to emerge weaker in retailing terms than equivalent continental cities. It remains to be seen whether we will ultimately follow the American path, with little comparison retailing remaining in town centres. Up to a point the decentralisation of comparison shopping can be tolerated by town centres, but beyond a certain point American style decline would follow.

We are some way from this point in 1987, but it is clearly on the horizon.

# Shop Location Analysis

David Rogers
*DSR Marketing Systems Inc*

*To base site selection methods on questions round a board room table such as "Is Hartlepool as nice as Wilmslow?" is clearly not enough. Retailers must be more thorough and organised about location procedures. Many have; but many, in the author's words, are still "winging it." There are a variety of techniques available for estimating turnovers and evaluating new sites; some of the principal approaches are described in this chapter.*

$S$hop development has become a more complex process during the 1980s. Gone are the days of High Street dominance, supposedly uni-dimensional consumers, and the *de facto* monopolies frequently conferred by the restrictive policies of Local Authority planners.

Instead, the 1980s have accentuated the insecurities of new retail development. For example:

— "Beggar my neighbour" planning policies in certain areas of the country have brought unexpected and severe new competition.

— New techniques are needed to appraise "out-of-town" sites instead of the traditional High Streets.

— "Targeted" retail concepts, such as Next, mean that it is no longer sufficient to know if there are "enough" people in a catchment area. Rather, the question is "are there enough of the right type."

— There is a shortage of sites for the large new stores offering the selection desired by today's car-borne shoppers.

Given this new climate, retailers must become more thorough and organised about their shop location procedures, and more accurate with turnover forecasts for new stores. Many have, such as Tesco and Sainsbury, but too many are still "winging it."

First, it must be appreciated that shop location procedures are more than just a method of estimating turnover. Rather, they represent the entire manner in which a retail management makes decisions about investing in a new store. At the very least, a shop location procedure should include the following steps:

1. One (or more) executive(s) should be made responsible for assembling the information on which management will base its decisions. Typically, this executive is someone in the firm's property department. Larger retail firms, however, may prefer the "independent view" of an executive who reports to somebody other than the Property Director.

2. Research should be conducted on the catchment areas, images and customer segments of *existing* stores that are broadly similar to

those under consideration. Without this data bank of information, sales forecasting for new stores cannot be accurate. This is particularly true for today's specialised retail concepts, where the "right" number of the "wrong" people can be disastrous.

The need for such a data bank is equally important, whether the firm prepares turnover estimates internally or uses an outside consultant to evaluate new sites.

3. A "site screening" analysis should be conducted before the time and money is spent on an in-depth location study. In other words, the "wheat should be separated from the chaff."

The need for site-screening methodology has increased in recent years in tandem with the increasingly sophisticated — and time consuming — techniques which are being applied to estimate turnovers. The desire of managements for greater accuracy in new store decision-making has inevitably meant that fewer sites can be reviewed in depth.

To "do the job" a site-screening method must be cheap and easy to do. Most retailers already have an informal sophisticated procedure. For example, "which Director shouts the loudest," "is Hartlepool as nice as Wilmslow," and "is the rent asked about our usual percentage norm"? However, more sophisticated methods of site-screening than these are now available!

4. If a site survives the screening process, it must then undergo an in-depth study, regardless of the time pressures imposed by estate agents or by any fears that a competitor "may take the site before we do." Management must remember the maxim: Act in haste; repent at leisure.

This analysis can be conducted internally or externally using a consultancy, and typically involves the use of the analogue, regression, or gravity modelling methods (see below).

Whatever the method of estimating turnover, however, a detailed location study should include the thorough evaluation of the following:

— Site characteristics,
— Road and street access patterns,
— The catchment area estimated for the proposed store,
— Catchment area population characteristics and trends,
— The local economic base, including unemployment levels, and
— Competition, both present and future.

These studies inevitably involve thorough fieldwork, take time and can be conducted only by an expert market analyst. This underscores the importance of having an in-house site screening method, so that detailed studies can be limited to those that are truly necessary *and* be done properly.

It is dumbfounding that the site analyst for one major UK retailer has gone on record as saying that a day trip is sufficient field time to evaluate an investment decision that might average £6 million per store for that retailer!

5. The obvious final step in a shop location procedure is a thorough financial analysis of the anticipated revenues, expenses and profits associated with the proposed store development. This step is the most crucial one in management's decision-making on a proposed store — but obviously rests on the quality of the data and judgements assembled in the preceding steps.

## Techniques available

Having outlined the *process* of shop location analysis, what techniques are available to retail managements? And how does a management select the best techniques and approaches for its needs?

In arriving at the "best" approach, some of the crucial questions for a management to ask itself are as follows:

1. How many existing stores do we have which are *similar* to those that will be developed in the future? This is the crucial "data base" of existing knowledge which influences the techniques that can be used by a retailer.

For example, a retailer with five shops cannot develop and employ a multiple turnover estimation model (which needs 30 stores or more before it can be developed).

It is also important to note the word "similar". There is little point in Asda (for example) studying the performance of 20,000 square feet supermarkets if all its plans to develop in the future are superstores in excess of 45,000 square feet.

2. Do we wish to use an outside consultancy, establish an in-house department, or a bit of both?

3. What is our investment risk in a new store? This obviously affects how much management should spend on its location analysis procedure, and the degree of precision required in estimating turnovers. For example, Benetton obviously has a different perspective on investment risk than J. Sainsbury.

77

4. What priority, resources and time can we give to shop location research *vis-a-vis* other management tasks and budget requirements? There is obviously no point in developing a complex, highly accurate procedure if the staff are not available to put it into effect. In this situation, a simpler procedure which *could* be carried out would be more effective.

5. What do we want the technique(s) to achieve? Approximate turnover ranges for site-screening purposes, precise turnover estimates, or the identification of promising market areas and locations?

6. Is our appeal to consumers heavily segmented — in which case multiple regression or discriminant analysis would be appropriate — or is it more narrowly based on convenience?

It is beyond the brief of this chapter to detail the various techniques of shop location analysis (for example, see Davies and Rogers, *Store Location and Store Assessment Research,* John Wiley, 1984). However, a brief listing is in order, starting with the simpler techniques:

The most basic approach is *demographic data analysis.* Are there enough people "around" a prospective site, and are they of the right type? This approach is obviously only adequate for the initial screenings of markets and sites but has become much easier in recent years through the services of data firms such as Pinpoint Analysis and CACI who have computerised the 1981 Census of Population.

Demographic reports can be generated for "custom" areas, such as a two-mile radius around a site, and can identify retail spending potential as well as population data and geo-demographic clusters, such as PIN and ACORN. Some reports also provide estimates of the numbers of stores of a given type that may be supported by the available spending. These "supportable store" estimates can then be compared with an actual field inventory of competitors to indicate whether there is the potential available for an additional store.

However, there are two main limitations to these reports. First, "you have to know what you are looking for." That is, wherever possible, existing stores (and customers) must be studied so that the catchment areas and customer segments to be served by new sites can be accurately estimated.

Secondly, the highly promoted cluster methods, such as ACORN and PIN, can be misleading if not carefully analysed. For example, if existing stores happen to have been located near a particular cluster group, the results of a geo-demographic analysis will show that this group is particularly "promising" for new stores, although, in fact, the relationship may merely reflect a coincidence of past location decisions. This weakness is not as great a problem for comparison goods retailers, such as clothing and shoe stores, since they draw trade over extensive distances. However, it can produce very misleading conclusions for convenience-oriented retailers, such as supermarkets and DIY stores.

The *Ratio Method* can provide a turnover estimate where no "similar" stores are yet in operation, as where an entirely new concept is planned. The method allocates sales to the proposed store in relation to its share of competing space (for the types of goods to be sold), and is a variant of the simple method used by many Local Authority planners.

The obvious weakness of the Ratio Method is that it does not consider the differing images of competing retailers and the resulting variations in their sales per square foot.

A major improvement over the Ratio Method, at least for those retailers having existing stores in operation, is the *Analogue Method*. This procedure involves measuring the market share performance and catchment areas of one or more existing stores and then the use of these data as "analogues" to arrive at turnover estimates for new stores.

### Market shares

New sites are matched against existing analogue stores and the market shares achieved by the latter are referred to in order to estimate the market shares that would be achieved by a new store. This reference process obviously involves careful adjustments for any differences in competition, population characteristics, and so on.

The analogue method therefore quantifies and reflects the unique image and performance of a retailer, may be used where there are only a few "analogue" stores in operation, and is simple and cheap to apply. Also, and very important in a dynamic field such as retailing, the analogue procedure can easily be re-developed for altered circumstances, such as a product range extension.

The key weak-point of the analogue method is the subjectivity involved in selecting the appropriate analogues for a new site, and in considering the inter-related impacts of competition, demographics and distance on the market shares and turnover likely to be achieved at a new location.

The search for less subjective forecasting methods has, therefore, produced considerable interest by retailers in statistical modelling techniques during the last twenty years. The most important of these have been multiple regression analysis, multiple discriminant analysis and gravity models. It is important to appreciate, however, that these modelling approaches can *reduce* the degree of subjectivity but *do not* remove it. Inevitably, they are simplifications of reality and are rarely comprehensive with respect to all the factors influencing the level of turnover at a new site. For example, specific site factors, such as poor visibility at a car park exit, are rarely included in models but can have a dramatic effect on turnover.

*Multiple regression* and *discriminant* analysis differ in that the former provides "precise" turnover estimates while the latter allocates new sites to turnover range categories, for example, under versus over one million pounds per year. However, the two techniques have much in common, particularly with respect to their strengths and limitations (please see Figure 1).

Expressed simply, the regression and discriminant models are produced from an analysis of existing store performances which identifies those variables (such as parking availability, competition, etc.) that are significantly correlated (positively or negatively) with variations in turnover from store to store. These key variables, and their associated equations, are then used to predict turnover at new sites (in the case of regression) or to allocate new sites to turnover ranges (in the case of discriminant analysis).

The major problem in developing and applying these models is their complexity and the fact that they need a rare blend of statistical expertise and a practical knowledge of retailing. Two scenarios have been all too common. First, regression modelling has, on occasion, been over-sold by data firms concerned to develop an in-built dependence on their data products. In the process, important statistical assumptions have been flouted in order to inflate the apparent reliability of the models. Secondly, academics with little understanding of retailing have been retained (often to save costs) and the resulting models have included variables which "fit" from a statistical point of view but in reality are weak (or irrelevant) predictors of what makes a good or bad shop location.

These problems can be reduced if the retailer remains fully

## Figure 1
## Regression and discriminant models: Key strengths and limitations

| Strengths | Limitations |
|---|---|
| Powerful for retailers with a highly segmented appeal. | Expensive to develop. |
| Provides an objective discipline for different market analysts to follow. | Need at least 30 relevant stores as a data base. |
| Easy to use once developed. No need for computer interaction in turnover forecasting | Must be entirely re developed for changed conditions. |
| Provides an evaluation of those existing stores used in the development of the model. | More than one model is frequently necessary (for different location types or areas of the country). |
| | Many important statistical assumptions must be observed. |

involved — and asks questions — at all stages in the development of a statistical sales forecasting model. There are no "black boxes", no one particular system that is the one and only approach. Each model is developed on the basis of many judgement calls and the retailer should be aware of them.

### A static picture

It is also important to appreciate that regression and discriminant models provide a *static* picture of store performance and the factors affecting it. Major changes in retail image, product ranges and competition will usually limit the "life" of these models to only three or four years, at which time they must be completely re-developed. Unfortunately, many retailers have invested £40,000 or more in regression-based site selection models without this knowledge.

Finally, *gravity models* have become increasingly popular in recent years for retail turnover forecasting, despite their fall from favour at Planning Inquiries and at the Department of the Environment.

A variety of "gravity models" are now available to retailers, some of them being quite dated formulations which are specially developed for each local catchment area. The newer, more powerful versions are size-distance computer programmes which forecast the turnover of a new store based on a simultaneous consideration of (a) store sizes and images (including those of competitors), (b) distance, and (c) population distribution and density. These models were developed through extensive research into store performances and how they are affected by different store sizes, location types, and competitive levels. That is, they rest on the summarised experience of a large number of analogues. The latter are organised into a set of disciplined procedures which reduce — but by no means remove — the chances of erroneous judgements.

The strengths and limitations of gravity models are summarised in Figure 2. A key quality of the gravity model, particularly in a mature sector of retailing, is that it offers a rapid "what if" capability for evaluating store development choices, such as alternative store sizes, formats, or locations. In addition, the method can simulate possible competitor reactions to the opening of a new store.

However, gravity models also have limitations, particularly their need for time-consuming data collection and complex computer interaction.

In using gravity model methods, retailers should again beware of any "black box" sales pitch and satisfy themselves that any "generic" model is fully adjusted to reflect the images and characteristics of their stores. This can only be accomplished through extensive research into the catchment areas and market share performances of existing stores *similar* to those which will be developed on the basis of the model's forecasts.

There are, therefore, a variety of techniques available to retailers for estimating turnovers and evaluating new sites. No one method is the "ideal approach" since each method has different strengths, limitations, and areas of application. Further, the "right" method for a retail firm will reflect its precise objectives and needs, and its "corporate culture." For example, an entrepreneurial firm in a rapid growth mode is unlikely to have the internal resources for a very sophisticated method to be effective. In addition, the probability of rapid changes in its store concept and in competition mean that it would be unwise to "over-invest" in sophisticated but static computer models. In this circumstance, a combination of the analogue method and demographic data analysis would be the most cost-effective approach.

Whatever the precise methods of shop location analysis adopted, they must be set within an organised management procedure for making decisions about new locations, *and* management must be fully involved in their development. Buying in a "black box" technique can led to obvious problems in practical application.

Further, as has been stressed, an improved shop location method must incorporate "homework" in terms of the market appeals and performances of *existing* stores. "Real work" is therefore involved in developing better methods of shop location analysis. However, in the competitive and insecure environment of the late 1980s those retailers who don't invest in this "insurance policy" are in grave danger of making increasingly expensive mistakes.

**Figure 2**
**Gravity models: Key strengths and limitations**

| Strengths | Limitations |
|---|---|
| Answers "what if" questions regarding different store sizes, images and locations. | Needs accurate method for estimating the turnover and/or attractiveness of competitors. |
| Estimates impacts on sister stores and competitors. | Needs reliable system for estimating consumer spending in local areas. |
| Relatively easy to re-develop for changed circumstances. | Relatively insensitive to demographic effects. |
| Flexible in application to different location types and areas of the country. | Needs time-consuming data collection and computer interaction for turnover estimates. |
| Particularly useful for (relatively) unsegmented convenience goods retailers. | |

# Trends in Physical Distribution

Tony Rudd

*Distributors should be concentrating their efforts on moving data, not lorries. A more professional approach is required to meet the scope and responsibilities of distribution; one answer to this is the National Materials Handling Centre's M.Sc course. And the trend to specialisation is leading to growing dependence on professional, third party distributors.*

$P$hysical distribution patterns in retailing have changed dramatically in recent years. The availability of new technology has enabled both manufacturers and retailers to tackle a wide range of mutual problems together. As a result, the distribution industry today is undergoing a process of radical transformation, the principal medium of change being centred on the rapid development and application of information technology. At the heart of this revolution is an appreciation of the maxim that, wherever possible, distributors should really concentrate their efforts on moving data, not lorries.

Transport costs have always been a major ingredient in the distribution cost profile, particularly in the fast-moving consumer goods field. Those charged with moving products from the point of manufacture/supply through to the supermarket shelves have been determined to reduce and contain those costs incurred during the distributive cycle. But costs alone have not been the only reason why information technology has been so enthusiastically welcomed in the distribution sector.

Above all, it has helped to rationalise the complex logistics of delivering so many different lines to the loading bays of the major stores. In the past — apart from the problems of urban congestion which this introduced — valuable selling space was taken up with storage and receiving bays in the High Street locations. The system was both inefficient and costly, with a distinct lack of control over the distribution process in that few — if any — could ever track or trace the progress of a pallet through the network.

Food retailers with their high volume, low margin business were the first to exploit the new opportunities to streamline arrangements. For them, the ideal future scenario in distribution support would be to check the store shelves by bar-code reading at the end of each day's trading. This information would then be fed via computerised ordering to a central warehouse run by the retailer. The order would then be picked overnight and delivered to the store the next day in roll pallets. Each pallet would be packed so that it could be sequentially unloaded directly onto the shelves according to the store layout. The order would therefore directly reflect what was sold the previous day.

This approach would centralise ordering at head office. It would also concentrate manufacturers' deliveries to a fewer number of drop points, enabling the retailers to ask for even better margins to reflect the lower distribution costs at the beginning of the chain. It also eliminates, or drastically reduces, the need for large stock rooms at the supermarket since goods can be transferred direct from vehicle to shelf. Finally, it reduces staffing levels because salesmen and stock-room personnel are no longer required.

Electronic point-of-sale was another link in the chain which was widely expected to revolutionise stock control and ordering within the distribution cycle. In reality, it has taken the grocery chains much longer to organise EPoS so that individual stores can confidently rely on the fact that what went out through the till was automatically re-ordered via a computer link to the central warehouse. However, it is expected that with over 2000 lines to control, EPoS in the supermarket business will reach its full potential by the mid-1990s.

Up until the late 1970s, the distribution function in retailing was primarily the concern of the supplier. Today, it is increasingly the large multiple groups — Sainsbury, Tesco, Marks & Spencer — which are dictating and dominating the way that goods move through the supply chain. In grocery retailing, over 60% of the market is currently controlled by just six retailers: a quarter of the market lies with Sainsbury (12.3%) and Tesco (12.0%), with the Dee Corporation (11.8%) and Argyll/Safeway (9%) close behind. As such, Sainsbury and Tesco have been among those major companies setting the distribution pace, investing in large centralised warehousing facilities to service their growing number of outlets which have no local storage amenities close by or on-site.

This growth of centralised warehousing, alongside the concentration of power among the 'Big Six', has been among the major influences affecting food distribution during the 1980s. Up until then — from the mid-1960s through to the late 1970s — around 70% of the UK's distribution activity was undertaken by manufacturers' own account transport fleets. Following on from this, most of the important advances in materials handling/storage technology and distribution know-how tended to emanate from the manufacture-supply side of the industry.

With the onset of the recession, the large multiples seized the opportunity of using their considerable buying power to influence — and eventually dictate — their own distribution arrangements. The whole basis of the supply chain shifted, with manufacturers meeting the retailers' delivery criteria, rather than vice versa. What this realignment emphasised was that, in future, the High Street retailer would become the public's buying agency, rather than the manufacturer's selling medium. This, in turn, introduced greater competitiveness amongst the retailers, who began to seek faster response times from their distribution networks, in addition to smaller, more frequent deliveries. Physical distribution had become part of the retailer's marketing strategy.

### Centralised warehousing

Those traditional distribution approaches outlined earlier — characterised by multi-vehicle drops from a wide range of suppliers, congestion, queuing, in-store stock rooms, and so forth — could not have coped with the increased service demands placed upon them. Hence the move to centralised warehouse structures, enabling store replenishment to be consolidated into a single delivery each day.

Benefits for the retailer in controlling his own centralised distribution facilities therefore embrace:

— Economies of scale in terms of warehouse accommodation.

— Increased handling efficiencies, allowing individual stores to be replenished more quickly and regularly.

— Lower stockholding in the store, providing additional selling space.

— Replenishment carried out on a daily demand basis, giving a faster stockturn and a greater availability of individual lines.

— Lower inventory levels, transferring the problem back to the manufacturer. This also results in a more efficient warehouse operation. The stock needed to support a group of retail outlets can be much smaller than the total of the stocks held in the individual stores under a decentralised system. This advantage is increased by the tendency for bulk discount rates to be strictly applied to unit load multiples.

— Other miscellaneous benefits cover such aspects as full vehicle

87

utilisation, precise scheduling and the avoidance of untimely delays. The growing awareness and understanding of physical distribution has led to several new requirements from this discipline.

1. *The need to formulate 'total distribution' strategies which combine all the individual elements of materials handling, storage and transport into a fully integrated logistics concept.* This will move beyond the traditional 'warehouse' and 'transport' roles to include such aspects as administration, systems development and, increasingly, to the purchasing and sales functions. Today's evolving distribution service is clearly far broader and more complementary to other business functions than has hitherto been recognised. For this reason, the acceptance and exploitation of distribution as a corporate activity is now rapidly advancing. While UK industry can boast a proficient team of transport, warehousing and distribution personnel at middle management level, their effectiveness could be considerably enhanced by the recognition, at board level, of the full implications of an integrated physical distribution management (PDM) function.

2. *For the reasons outlined above, a more professional approach is required to meet the growing scope and responsibilities of the distribution department.* Here the National Materials Handling Centre at Cranfield is making a valuable contribution to training the country's future distribution executives. The Centre's M.Sc course in Distribution Technology and Management is claimed to be totally unique with no parallel at either undergraduate or post graduate level. The objectives of the course are to develop distribution specialists with a depth of technical knowledge over a wide range of areas and with management skills to enable full use to be made of the broader distribution approach. Other short courses on PDM are also offered by the NMHC.

3. *Greater flexibility to achieve the higher levels of service, dictated by shorter lead times, lower inventory holding and changing user requirements as company mergers and acquisitions give rise to new retail trading strategies.* This requirement probably accounts for the dramatic increase in third-party distribution services in recent years. Here the philosophy holds that we live in an era of specialisation: let the manufacturers concentrate on production, leave the retailers to run their stores and place the distribution function in the hands of professional, third-party distributors.

The trend to third-party distribution has been boosted in recent years by the development of a wide range of specialised services accommodating, for example, hanging garments, frozen or temperature controlled products, fragile goods, and so forth, as well as the more general consolidation services run by other leading contractors.

## Significant benefits

Retail customers contracting to the distribution services are offered a number of significant benefits:

(i) Considerable medium and short-term flexibility within the context of a rapidly changing retail distribution scene. The third-party contractor can adapt his operation more readily to meet the varied needs of a large mix of customers. Changes in service levels may be accomplished more easily if they do not entail investment decisions about a company's own distribution facilities.

(ii) Off-balance sheet financing which permits exclusive use of capital-intensive resources. This is especially important given the high investment levels in new retail stores.

(iii) A wide choice of options and a valuable insurance in the field of industrial relations. User companies are less vulnerable to strike action.

(iv) Economies of scale, especially in the areas of vehicle utilisation and in computers, materials handling aids and storage systems where, below a certain threshold scale of operation, unit distribution costs can rise sharply.

(v) An ability to exploit the transport expertise found in the manufacturing and transport sectors which is not so strongly represented within retailing. Furthermore, the third-party distributor employs specialist, skilled labour involved exclusively in the distribution task, backed up by first-class management and training geared specifically to the PD discipline.

4. *Technological innovation to meet the demands of the increasingly sophisticated distribution networks.* The overall aim of the distribution system is making the right product in the right quantities available in the right place at the right time. Viewed in this light, it is the key link between manufacturing and demand creation with a profound effect on the success or otherwise of both activities and therefore on the final profitability of an organisation.

It is not surprising therefore that considerable technological developments have been centred on this function in recent years, with particular emphasis on information transfer. Two aspects are paramount: firstly, control over the physical movement of goods and, secondly, control over the flow of information.

While there has been a dramatic increase in the application of computers to PD control procedures in the UK, British management can make even greater use of their diverse facilities. It is not simply a question of employing computers for such aspects as vehicle scheduling or transport routes, but applying them to the more difficult areas of assessment and judgement to give management a continuous monitoring of the total distribution network, both in terms of cost and performance.

Within distribution organisations, computers are now being used in four main areas: planning and simulation; information supply; operational control; and process control. Some of the most interesting developments have been in planning. Here, specialist programs can be useful, for instance, in vehicle route planning; in the strategic planning of distribution networks, covering the number and location of warehouse operations, where they investigate the capital and operating costs associated with alternative equipment and layout strategies. Another interesting planning program is aimed at assessing unit load efficiency.

Process-control computers have also accompanied some of the more dramatic innovations in warehousing hardware. This includes developments such as highbay automated storage and retrieval systems (AS/RS) for palletised unit loads, carousel picking systems, conveyors and parcel sorting systems, guidance networks for automated guided vehicles (AGVs), and perhaps eventually the use of robotics for various materials handling functions.

In AS/RS applications, a fundamental feature is that the computer tracks every pallet movement at each stage through the warehousing cycle — whether in storage, on the stacker crane or on the conveyor. The stock and pallet queue files of the warehouse computer keep this information updated for every movement. This is the real-time aspect of the modern distribution operation.

Emphasis on stock and the way it is moved has a direct bearing on the warehouse design. If the role of the warehouse is fully appreciated within the overall logistics framework, one can then begin to define those areas of advanced technology — such as automation, wire-guided systems and highbay configurations — which are relevant to future operations. But the functional requirements of the distribution warehouse must be clearly understood before there is any commitment to high levels of investment in advanced systems. In other words, technology for technology's sake should be avoided.

The appraisal of the unit cost of any item in the distribution chain is absolutely essential and must take precedence over considerations of technically advanced, capital intensive handling systems which do not provide that minimum cost criterion for the future.

The requirements of automation are that one must have:
— the type of traffic which can benefit from automation
— the volume of business to meet the high initial cost of the investment
— a computer or systems capability equal to the technological step one is taking in the warehouse development.

Generally speaking, the hardware for the storage function has kept pace with — if not ahead of — the requirements of the distribution networks.

## The narrow aisle concept

Although height is no longer regarded as the answer to all warehousing problems, the high-rise, narrow aisle concept — and all the equipment developments emanating from it — has had a greater impact on storage systems, in a shorter space of time, than any parallel warehousing advance.

The high-rise approach has totally altered the distribution industry's view of the warehousing function. High-rise can now be an integral part of the manufacturing process, an active dispenser of goods rather than a static holding aid. Add cladding to the racks, place a roof over the top, and you have a warehouse.

Add computer control, and you have a multi-purpose tool for which storage is only one of the many possible justifications for its existence. Without doubt, the narrow aisle installation is still one of the biggest single areas of future development in retail distribution, especially here in the UK where industry has been slower to invest in such systems when compared, for example, to West Germany, Japan and the USA.

In warehousing terms, what we are witnessing is a positive manifestation of that 'systems approach' to the distribution of goods. This is a marked change from the previously held view that warehousing is an inevitable and necessary evil. Today, distribution personnel assert that, correctly managed, 'materials flow' can result in *increased* manufacturing output, driver/vehicle productivity and sales; *reduced* stocks, control costs, energy consumption, etc; and — on a wider business front — *improved* industrial and community relations.

Other materials handling developments have been well documented and include:

— the fully automated narrow aisle truck: what was previously billed as the 'narrow aisle compromise' adopted by UK companies, is now seen as a sound and economic alternative — an approach, moreover, which is less capital intensive and more flexible in its operation than stacker cranes and which should become increasingly evident in retail distribution systems during the coming decade;

— automated guided vehicles (AGVs).

The development of data transfer to these types of guided trucks has opened up considerable scope for their increased utilisation in both the horizontal and vertical movement of palletised loads within the distribution warehouse.

Automated storage/retrieval systems and AGVs are just two examples of the new technology which is introducing new levels of skill to distribution practices. However, while such systems are now widely available, most distribution specialists in the UK agree that the country still falls some way behind many of its overseas competitors when it comes to adopting such operations.

A major reason for this is finance. While many manufacturers, suppliers and retailers would like to embark on automated programmes, the financial community is often reluctant to accept the benefits of automation in other than labour and land costs. The same people also look for a short-term return on investment and are therefore doubtful about supporting the substantial sums required for warehouse automation. Generally speaking, financial institutions still prefer backing the development of multi-purpose warehouse structures which can be adapted to other uses should the original activity be discontinued, rather than invest in more purpose-built facilities.

As in so many other sectors, this attitude by the City is hampering the full development of the retail distribution industry. Broadly speaking, warehouse developments tend to end up as compromise solutions involving various trade-offs between the use of space, inventory considerations and the need to maintain high service levels. As a result, the majority of modern UK warehouse installations still tend to opt for the narrow aisle compromise rather than the fully automated solution.

The distribution industry has reacted positively to the marked changes in both consumer habits and the development of the logistics infrastructure — changes epitomised by the new groupings in the retail trade and the emergence of out-of-town shopping locations, allied to the development of the commercial vehicle, the private car and the road network. Further development will no doubt continue apace in the years ahead and it is important that future expansion of the retail sector and its supporting distribution network should always take full account of environmental considerations and the legitimate needs and interests of the community which it serves.

In the final analysis, the health and well being of the environment will reflect the health of the country, which in turn will underline the achievements of the retail, manufacturing and distributive sectors.

# Convenience stores

David Kirby
*St David's University College, University of Wales*

*The move towards large-scale retailing which has characterised the retail sector over the past decade has been matched by the development of small convenience stores at the other end of the spectrum — the polarisation theory. Similarly, the emergence of a divided nation has generated an increasingly large market segment consisting of relatively money-poor/time-rich consumers. Characterised by unemployment, early retirement and increased age their shopping pattern is typically one of small, individual, value for money purchases.*

The changes which have taken place in British retailing over the past 10 to 15 years have been likened elsewhere to the changes occurring in manufacturing as part of the Industrial Revolution. In particular, the increase in the scale and form of production can be likened to the increased scale of retail operations and the adoption of mass merchandise techniques, while the concentration of manufacturing power has parallels with the continued concentration of retailing and the increasing dominance of the multiples.

If the analogy is correct, then as the Industrial Revolution took many decades to run its course, so it will be many years before the retail revolution is complete. Thus it is to be expected that before the end of the century further radical and innovative changes will have taken place in the form, organisation and location of retailing. Whatever the precise nature of these changes, it seems inevitable that the increasing polarisation of British retailing will continue, at least for the foreseeable future (Kirby, 1982).

In the past 10 or 15 years, retail polarisation has been a characteristic of the distributive systems of most high-level, western-style economies. The British retail system has been no exception, though the rate of polarisation has been slower, perhaps, than elsewhere and than might have been anticipated. Based on developments in the American retail system in the 1960s and early 1970s, it has been possible to formulate a theory of retail polarisation. This predicts that as stores get larger, numerically fewer and spatially more concentrated, so there emerges an increased need for small stores conveniently located close to the consumer's place of residence.

What the theory is suggesting, therefore, is that whereas the small manufacturing unit was replaced by the large-scale factory, the retail revolution is creating the conditions under which small-scale retailing can survive and prosper. At one end of the spectrum, the large retail operation (often part of a large, complex national or even international business organisation) will dominate the market, satisfying those consumer segments (the majority) which are highly mobile and able and prepared to shop in bulk.

At the other extreme will be the small, efficient retail operation (often, though not always part of a national or regional organisation) which satisfies the majority shopping needs of a consumer minority (i.e. those segments unable or unwilling to shop at large stores), plus the minority needs of the consumer majority. For this latter group, the small, local store is used for "topping up" — for the purchase of forgotten or out-of-stock items, for perishables or for "emergency" items.

To some, the changes which are likely to take place in British retailing between now and the end of the century are seen as part of a second retailing revolution. For them, this second revolution is likened to "the post-industrial or 'third-wave' revolution in manufacturing which is de-massifying the factory and tending towards shorter production runs based on flexible high technology" (Birchall, 1987, p.8).

The main weakness in this argument would seem to be that for the foreseeable future in Britain, there will continue to be an increase in the scale of both retail stores and retail organisations. Even so, the supporters of this line of reasoning are agreed that this second "revolution in retailing will see the rise of many small retailers, gearing their sales to a highly localised market" (op.cit. pp 8 & 9).

Thus, for whatever reason, convenience appears to be a characteristic of the changing face of British retailing. Indeed, the results of a consumer survey undertaken by Harris International Marketing have revealed that whereas in 1980 only 30 per cent of all consumers decided where to shop on the basis of convenience considerations, by 1985 the proportion had risen to 59 per cent. In contrast, price considerations had declined from 55 per cent in 1980 to only 35 per cent in 1985. This being the case, it would seem that the market opportunities for convenience trading are considerable and increasing. The question is, what constitutes "convenience."

When considering convenience, the tendency is to think in terms of location — the convenience of proximity. This being the case, the most convenient type of retail outlet is the traditional local corner store. However, convenience is much more than just proximity — it relates to access, to hours of trading, to the product range, etc. Accordingly, it has been argued, that "superstores outscore local corner shops every time in terms of convenience" (Gildersleeve, 1986, p.56).

Given their preferred locations and the provision of ample parking facilities, such stores are usually readily accessible, particularly for those with cars. To overcome the inconvenience of location for those without cars, bus services are often provided, while late night trading, usually two or three evenings a week, is provided for the convenience, in particular, of those without access to a car, and those unable to shop, during the working day. What is more, such stores carry, invariably, a product range which makes "one stop" convenience and, even, comparison shopping a possibility.

## A specialist retail format

In recognition of these various aspects of convenience, the convenience store has evolved as a specialist retail format satisfying, as mentioned earlier, the minority needs of the consumer majority and the majority needs of a consumer minority. Basically, the format involves trading from locations which provide easy access for the local community, over extended opening times and through a wide range of high demand products. Accordingly, a typical definition of a convenience store might be:

"A self-service store, usually between 1,000 and 3,000 sq. ft. located close to housing, with some parking facilities, offering a wide range of goods including grocery and CTN products, chemist sundries, alcohol and possibly other lines including video hire, fast foods or petrol, opening long hours including Sundays." (Verdict, 1986, p.4).

Convenience Stores originated in the United States. Some suggest that the first American convenience stores developed in the 1920s but by 1957 there were only just over 500. Between 1960 and 1974, the number increased from 2,500 to 22,700 and by 1980 there were something in the order of 36,000. Since then, growth has been extremely rapid. Current estimates suggest that there might be as many as 60,000 and the sector remains one of the fastest growing areas of American retailing.

From America, the concept has diffused to various other countries and the convenience concept is now well established in the retail systems of Australia and Japan as well as several European countries, including Sweden, Denmark (Gammond, 1985) and France. Thus the concept has been adopted world-wide, though it was not until the mid 1970s that it first appeared in Britain where it is still in an embryonic form, with only about 2,200 stores in 1986, and adoption has been less rapid than might have been anticipated. Indeed, it was not until the mid 1980s that a distinctive convenience store sector could be identified in the British retail system (Kirby, 1986). Even so, the sector is not homogenous.

**Table 1. British Convenience Store by Type, 1986**

| Type | Leading Companies | Estimated Number of Outlets |
|------|-------------------|------------------------------|
| Specialist Chains | Sperrings*, M&W, 7-Eleven, Circle K | 200 |
| Grocery Stores** | Eight Till Late, Late Stop, Lalani, Europa, Cullens, Eversheds | 1,533 |
| CTN Stores | Star News Shops, Forbuoys, Corners, One Stop, Clements | 88 |
| Forecourt Shops | Shopstop, Star Food Shop, Food Plus, Ultra Spar, Jiffy | 184 |
| | | 2,005 |

Source: Verdict, 1986.
*Taken over by Circle K.
**Excludes Co-op which operates some 20 or more Late Late Supershops as CWS franchises and is set to expand its convenience store operations (Gammond, 1986).

As table 1 demonstrates, perhaps as many as three-quarters of Britain's convenience stores are grocery outlets which have converted to the convenience store format. The main reason for this has been the influence of the voluntary groups, though even here enthusiasm for the concept has not been uniform and the 1,150 Spar Eight Till Late outlets represent some 85 per cent of the total number of symbol-led stores. Even so, despite the scepticism within the trade and the disappointing performance of organisations such as Cullens, the convenience store format has proved successful for many small, independent grocery businesses.

Specialist convenience store operators account for, perhaps, only 10 per cent of the total number of stores and although the four leading specialist chains increased their outlets by 30 per cent in 1985/86 alone, it is generally accepted that this particular sector has not grown at the rate which might have been predicted.

There are several reasons for this. They include the shortage of both suitable sites and appropriate management skills, difficulties over the recruitment of franchisees, geographical variations in both consumer acceptance and the enforcement of the restrictions on Sunday trading, failure to appreciate the major infrastructural differences between the British and overseas markets and, finally, the controls on the distribution of newspapers and magazines.

## Conversion of CTNs

Since newspapers and magazines are an important element in the product mix of the typical convenience store, it is comparatively easy for an existing CTN business to adopt a convenience store format. Even so, relatively few CTNs trade as convenience stores at present, possibly reflecting the slower rate of closures in this sector compared with, for example, the grocery trade. Recent trends suggest, however, that the rate of conversion is increasing and Verdict (1986, p. 15) anticipates "much more activity in the convenience area from CTNs in the future". With the declining profitability of petrol sales, the major oil companies are beginning to recognise the potential for forecourt trading and to follow their counterparts overseas.

This involves moving away from the restricted product mix and trading methods of the traditional service station outlet to the broader product range of the convenience store, and several oil companies have linked up with existing convenience store operators (e.g. Ultramar Oil and Spar, Elf with Spar and VG, Murco and Misselbrook & Weston and Sperrings and Total Oil).

With in excess of 20,000 sites in the UK, it could be that the "convenience store with pumps" will become as characteristic, in Britain, as it is in certain other countries. In this respect it is interesting to observe that in March 1987, a special package for the independent service station operator was launched by Maceline, a symbol group which, until then, had taken a somewhat cautious approach to convenience store trading.

In America, the convenience store format is at least 30-years-old and it has not yet reached the end of its life-cycle. In Britain, it is no more than 10. This would suggest that, despite the slower than anticipated rates of growth, there is considerable scope for further development, especially when it is appreciated that it is only now that the level of polarisation is being reached which is required to create the market opportunities for convenience store development. Despite the decades of small shop closures and the rapid growth, during the late 1970s/early 80s, of hypermarkets and superstores, Britain has remained over-shopped when compared with countries like the United States.

In 1982 the UK had 54,230 outlets compared with 183,500 in the USA. If it had a density of shop provision equal to that of the USA (i.e. 0.82 outlets per 1,000 population), it would have 44,513 — i.e. a decline of 9,717 outlets. (Source: Nielsen, 1982).

Thus it would seem that, for the foreseeable future, further closures will take place in the small shop sector and the development of large stores will continue, albeit at a rate somewhat slower than has occurred in the past. Such conditions will create the environment in which the efficiently-managed, correctly-located convenience store operation can survive and flourish.

Under such circumstances, it might be expected that the number of convenience stores would increase, as would their share of the retail market. Given the paucity of the official data base, it is difficult to predict with any accuracy, though estimates by Euromonitor in 1985 suggest that by 1990 there will be some 4,200 outlets with a £1.7 billion turnover representing a 1.3 per cent share of the retail market. This compares with some 2,500 outlets with a turnover of £1 billion and a market share of 0.9 per cent in 1987. (Source: Euromonitor).

Despite the slower than anticipated rate of growth, the difficulties surrounding Sperrings and 7-Eleven, the withdrawal of Majik Markets from the UK, and the trading difficulties experienced by Cullens, the convenience store will become an important element in the British retail system.

Not only is the system itself, through polarisation, creating the conditions under which the efficient small store can survive, but the market, also, is changing. The emergence of what is frequently termed a "divided nation" is breaking down the largely single-class,

100

mass consumption market which has characterised post-war Britain. With increased unemployment, early retirement and an ageing population there is emerging an increasingly large market segment consisting of relatively money-poor/time-rich consumers. In marketing terms, these are the "Frontier Consumers" (Blackwell and Talarzyk, 1983) whose shopping behaviour is characterised by small, individual, value for money purchases. At the other extreme are the "Sybaritic consumers" — the growing superclass segment made up of young, upwardly mobile professionals (Yuppies) and double income households, frequently without children (Dinkies) — whose shopping decisions are based on considerations of quality, prestige, style and convenience.

## Mass consumption market

Both segments afford distinct and growing opportunities for the convenience store, as does the traditional mass-consumption market, providing the needs of the different segments are identified, clearly, and the appropriate positioning strategy is adopted, correctly.

In this context it is interesting to observe that Cullens has targetted the sybaritic segment (Sharples, 1985). This is the first time such a focused strategy has been adopted but since the launch in July 1985, the concept has been modified considerably and the company profit levels have been lower than anticipated. However, this does not belie the appropriateness of the strategy. The successful operators "will be those operators that get right both the format and the location" (Kirby, 1986, p. 12).

As with Cullens, the whole convenience store sector in Britain is having to learn from experience, irrespective of whether it is an indigenous British operation or one with experience of convenience store retailing overseas. Once this initial learning phase is over, the convenience store will emerge as an important growth format and, as was predicted over a decade ago, small store retailing will re-emerge as an integral element in the changing face of British retailing.

## References

Birchall, J. (1987). *Save Our Shop: the Fall and Rise of the Small Co-operative Store*. Manchester, Holyoake Books.

Blackwell, R. D., and Talarzyk, W. W. (1983). Lifestyle Retailing: Competitive Strategies for the 1980s. *Journal of Retailing*. Winter, 7-27.

# The Changing Face of British Retailing

Euromonitor (1985). *Convenience Stores*. London, Euromonitor Publications Ltd.

Gammond, J. (1985). Continental Cousins. *Convenience Store*. November 1, 39-40.

Gammond, J. (1986). Opening All Hours. *Convenience Store*. May 30, 23.

Gildersleeve, J. (1986). More than a Nation of Shopkeepers. *Retail Planning and Development*, London, PTRC Education and Research Services Ltd.

Kirby, D. A. (1982). Retailing in the Age of the Chip. *Service Industries Review*, 2, 1, 9-21.

Kirby, D. A. (1986). Convenience Stores: the Polarisation of British Retailing. *Retail and Distribution Management*. March/April 1986, pp. 7-12.

Nielsen (1982). *The Grocery Marketing Scene: a Nielsen worldwide review of significant industry trends*. Oxford, A. C. Nielsen Company Ltd.

Sharples, S. (1985). Cullen's: The c-store for the sophisticates. *Retail and Distribution Management*. November/December 1985, pp. 24-27.

Verdict (1986). *Verdict on Convenience Stores*. London, Verdict Research Ltd.

# The Changing Consumer

Michael Poynor
*College for the Distributive Trades*

*No retailer is going to be entirely successful unless he understands his market properly. To do that he needs to have a clear idea of the consumer he is aiming at, and today those consumers are very different from those of the '60s or even the '70s. The youth market is finished; purchasing power now lies with the 25-40-year-olds, whilst the most affluent sector is that of the 45-59-year-olds. And now in the late 1980s the north/south divide, with all that that implies in terms of regional and social inequalities, is likely to be more significant than ever.*

# The Changing Face of British Retailing

$\big)$ $\mathrm{T}$he changing face of British retailing is both a reflection of, and a response to, fundamental changes in the consumer marketplace. Whether British consumers are changing more radically or more rapidly than before is uncertain. However, the speed and detail with which changes in consumer profiles are being captured by increasingly sophisticated information systems mean that retailers know more about their customers and more quickly than ever.

But does this make them easier targets? No. For the refinement in client groupings — (CACI, for example, analyse "enumeration districts" of 150 households throughout the country) — and the outmoding of conventional terms of customer classifications by class or socio-economic group alone, often result in highlighting the complexities and the contradictions of consumer behaviour rather than in pinpointing market potential.

The statistical study of human population is still the main underpinning dimension of the marketplace. The statistics, which emanate mainly from the Office of Population Censuses and Surveys, may be grouped under the headings of Age; Income; Families & Households; Employment; Unemployment; and Geo-demographics; with gender analysis relevant throughout. It is useful to consider recent and predicted trends for each in turn with the overall projection of a 4½ per cent increase in the British population to 52.2 million by the end of the century.

Baby booms cause deep undulations to swell across predictive age structure graphs. Yet these graphs are perhaps the easiest to assess; all people in 1995 (say) or eight years old or more have obviously already been born. The Henley Centre for Forecasting (HCF) — a goldmine of consumer information — recently produced the following chart (1). It is clear from this that the youth markets which have been the linchpin of many successful retail ventures in recent years will soon go into a sharp decline. Conversely, large growth can be forecasted in the prime young adult sector, the so-called "2CV 2TV"

**Percentage Change in the Age Structure
of the Population 1985-1995**

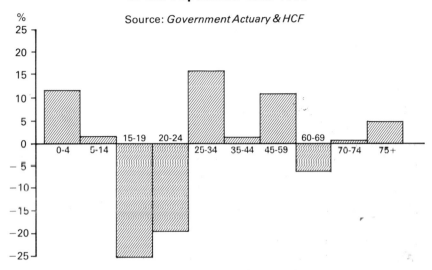

generation. This is, however, a hybrid group as it embraces young parents in their thrifty nests as well as those celebrated childless acronyms "dinkies" and "oinks" whose disposable income will demand much attention.

But so will disposable nappies! Fertility rates (surely one of the hardest statistics to predict with precision) will also show a significant rise on the back, as it were, of the increase in the 25-34-year-old sector. Mothercare, currently the underachiever of the Storehouse Group, is reported to be pinning its hopes on "SmartyPants", a new disposable nappy "which the Group is confident will take 10 per cent of a market expected to grow to £400 million a year". (*The Independent,* 3 May, 1987.)

Traditionally, the most affluent sector is that of the 45-59-year-olds. Peak pre-retirement salaries, paid-up mortgages, empty nests, sums of inheritance, greater leisure time (as well as increasingly generous early retirement packages), all add up to a rich seam of discretionary spending levels, sometimes irreverently referred to as "grey power"! Retailers of luxury products and travel and leisure goods for example, should do particularly well over the next decade as will, no doubt, suppliers of senior health care and medication. Investment and other financial services should also prosper.

The Economic Intelligence Unit (EIU) forecasts an average annual growth in real incomes of 3.3 per cent to 1990 and in consumer spending of 3.7 per cent (*Retail Business,* May 1987). The disparity between these two figures can partially be explained by a reduction in savings ratios and a strong rise in consumer credit. But that's not the whole story.

There are other less documented factors currently influencing the disproportionately high levels of consumer spending. One is "personal portfolio adjustment", ie the fact that debt has become more socially acceptable under its name of credit and that householders are more inclined to increase their overall levels of indebtedness. The other is equity withdrawal, or "mortgage lending leakage". This refers to the practice, prevalent in some parts of the country — notably the South East — whereby escalating property values exploit unlimited mortgage availability with some consumer spending being financed from paper gains in real estate; in short, the disposable capital syndrome!

Government tax cuts and lower interest rates have boosted retail sales in a fairly conventional manner, but shareholding profits are, for many, a newer source of income. The number of shareholders in the UK has grown from 3 million in 1979 to 8.5 million in 1986 (according to a recent *NOP* survey). However, the sizeable (c100 per cent) profits made from the shares, for example, of British Telecom and British Gas have seen the number of their shareholders decline in total from 6.6 million to approximately 4.9 million.

Changing social attitudes to income, earned and unearned, have become a hallmark of Conservative Britain in the 1980s; profit and money are no longer dirty words in most circles and "Going for it" has become the Yuppy motto par excellence!

## Shareholding profits

Although personal wealth has become more evenly distributed in recent years, nonetheless, virtually all wealth is owned by just 50 per cent of the population with the top 10 per cent owning half. The composition and circumstances of family groups and households within the invidious socio-economic divisions of the "Haves" and "Have nots" are crucial pieces of information for retail marketeers. And there is no shortage of source material.

Gerard O'Neill, a senior business analyst at The Henley Centre, wrote recently in *Marketing* (17 May, 1987) about two key dimensions viz "the amount of income and wealth generated by the economy and the extent to which some groups of consumers benefit more than others". Clear definition of these groups is thus a priority task.

Despite a modern revolution in many domestic arrangements, the majority of people still live in a family context. However, divorces have more than doubled from 80,000 in 1971 to 175,000 in 1985, that figure itself showing an 11 per cent increase over the year before — a result, perhaps, of the Matrimonial and Family Proceedings Act (1984) which now allows couples to petition for divorce after just one year of marriage. Statistics from the OPCS show, at the same time, that the birthrate has increased, with live births occuring inside marriage up by 1 per cent in 1985, but with those occuring outside marriage up by 14 per cent; the latter (totalling 126,000 last year) now account for one in five of all births. Nearly 12 per cent of dependent children now live in a single parent family.

There are, notwithstanding, on average 400,000 marriages a year in Britain. Yet despite this strong undercurrent of continuing belief in conventional family values across generations, the number of households has increased at the direct expense of their average size. Professor William Wilkie of the University of Florida in a recent book entitled *"Consumer Behaviour"* (John Wiley & Sons 1986) remarks: "A substantial proportion of all consumption involves the shared use of products and services. Most houses and apartments are shared. In turn, so are many of the products and services consumed therein". It follows that the explosion in household numbers over the past two decades will have seen in some product/service categories a disproportionately greater increase in consumer spending than the increase in population would suggest.

Consumer research must not ignore the family as a consuming unit in our society. "The family not only makes purchases, it also influences children in their approaches to consumer behaviour in the future" (Professor Wilkie). However, it is not easy to relate the dynamics of varying family life cycles to specific market demands unless one considers the role of the breadwinner or, rather, breadwinners.

It is the growth in women's employment and the incidence of dual-earner families (57 per cent of Britain's married couples) that has had the greatest impact on social structures and consumer spending in recent years. The number of women in paid employment has gradually increased to stand currently at 9.7 million, whilst the number of men has declined to 11.9 million (HCF). This trend of *rapprochement* will surely continue but it should disguise neither the imbalance of female part-time employees over male full-timers, nor the on-going inequities of pay. It is not just the contribution made by married women's employment to family purchasing potential that needs to be considered, it is the discretion and autonomy of expenditure which women enjoy from their independent earnings. Working mothers this year have over £12 billion available in disposable income from earnings and family benefits, with full-time women workers last year earning in total some £35 billion. When demographics join forces with labour economics retailers must respond.

### The "dinki" phenomenon

Childless couples, in or out of wedlock but both in work, constitute of course one of the highest spending household groups. The "dinki" phenomenon (dual income, no kids) is no mere media fad; it's very big business. 4.3 million couples below retirement age without dependent children but with an estimated disposable income of £65 billion this year, make one of Britain's most important demographic groups. Add to this the spending power of marginal groups such as "single-gender-couples" (whose "pink pounds" represent an unmeasured though sizeable tranche of consumer spending) and one's out of the ball park!

Yet how can retailers translate consumer dynamics into trading policies? What are the implications for range-building and the provision of customer services which result from phenomena as diverse as working mothers with new priority needs for convenience and time-saving to early retirement entrepreneurs (effectively middle-aged pensioners) who are comparatively young and healthy individuals with opportunities and challenges that require a retail response?

Before these questions can be addressed there is the major issue of unemployment to be considered and, linked to this, some social and regional polarisations which tend to make most generalisations on consumer demand inaccurate or even inflammatory.

Perhaps the most worrying statistic within the unemployment

figures (which in their own right cause anxiety enough at the current level of c.3 million) is that over two-fifths of the unemployed labour force have been unemployed for more than a year. A major consequence of this has, of course, been to polarise the jobs' market into those with and those without.

But it goes further. The Henley Centre sees a dual labour force at work which it classfies as "insiders" and "outsiders". The former, workers with secure, regular employment, have considerable influence over their level of wages and conditions of work. It is worth noting, for example, that the average annual hours worked in the UK has decreased over the past 10 years by eight per cent. The "outsiders" have a more precarious hold on their jobs (often with temporary or part-time contracts) and are competing with the unemployed for peripheral work. Although not all part-time work should be seen in a negative light — many mothers, for example, find it ideal — the share of part-timers now stands at 21.2 per cent of the total in the UK, a significantly higher percentage than in most other countries.

The net result of job insecurity and, even worse, the threat or actuality of unemployment on the consumer market-place has been to squeeze the middle. There is a resultant "schizophrenia" which, according to the Henley Centre, is likely to prevail for some time. Its effect has been for the majority — the more affluent population — to move into low volume, higher value-added markets and for the worse off minority to opt for high volume, lower value-added markets. One only has to examine recent changes in range development and store refurbishment on and beyond the High Street to see how resolutely the retailers have gone "up-market". ASDA, for example, whose original success was founded on an unashamedly proletarian formula, has recently introduced into its Fresh Produce department a range of recherché goods under the label "Exotica". The Henley Centre reckons that the pendulum of market share has swung significantly with Britain's top 20 per cent of households (numbering some four million) increasing their slice of the action by £6-£7 billion net over the past decade at the expense of the bottom sector.

There is much talk of the "Two Nations" phenomenon, and some of the evidence is, indeed, incontrovertible: almost 2.8 million people were living below the supplementary benefit line in 1983 against under 2.1 million in 1979. But is the "North/South Divide" as accurate a tag?

The techniques of linking population types to the areas in which they live is an important marketing tool and one which has spawned a number of increasingly finely-tuned data systems in recent years. Its importance is obvious. *Where* the customers are is as crucial as *Who* they are. It is particularly useful, of course, for direct marketing and mail order, undeniably areas of dynamic growth potential.

## Prosperity levels

Geodemographics have been used especially to plot inter-regional migration patterns which act as a fair barometer of prosperity levels across the country. There have, in fact, been some quite dramatic shifts through an on-going mood of "ruralisation". Since 1979 there has been a net exodus of half a million people from metropolitan areas to suburban or rural areas. Populations of the North, North-West, Yorkshire and Humberside will decline by five per cent by the year 2000 — but so too will Greater London. Over the same period the South-West, South East and East Anglia are expected to increase their population levels by as much as 10 per cent.

This would appear to support the argument that a North/South Divide does indeed exist. However, inner city deprivation is worse in London than in any of its Northern counterparts. A recent publication by the Low Pay Unit entitled "Poverty and Labour in London" claims that the disposable income of London's poorest 10 per cent of households fell by more than 23 per cent between 1983 and 1985, that 1.8 million Londoners are estimated to be living on the poverty margin and that between 1971 and 1985 half a million jobs have been lost in the capital. New-found Yuppy affluence and Big Bang's transfiguration of London's Docklands throw such statistics into the starkest contrast.

The myth of an absolute North/South Divide is further exploded by another recent publication: "Regional policy — the Way Forward". This Employment Institute pamphlet makes two key observations:

i) An analysis of unemployment by individual electoral wards suggests that unemployment experience can vary more between housing estates within a mile or two of each other than it does from one end of the country to the other.

ii) Housing costs are much lower outside the South East leaving more spending money in the pocket. This is why retailers have long regarded many Northern cities as containing some of the best prime High Street sites.

Linked to the question of migration is the issue of mobility, for which car ownership levels and drive-time analyses provide crucial pieces of information. Ours is clearly a four wheeled future. The majority of households have owned their own car since the late 1960s and, in more recent years, the proportion of households owning two or more cars has doubled to 18 per cent. It will come as no surprise, therefore, to see on the EIU chart (Table 2) that cars represent one of the strongest areas of predicted consumer spending over the next few years.

**Table 2**
**Major Items of Consumer Spending, 1985-90**
*£bn at 1990 prices*

|  | Actual | | Forecast | | | |
|---|---|---|---|---|---|---|
|  | **1985** | **1986** | **1987** | **1988** | **1989** | **1990** |
| Durables |  |  |  |  |  |  |
| Cars | 8.0 | 8.6 | 9.5 | 10.1 | 10.3 | 10.7 |
| Furniture and carpets | 3.6 | 3.7 | 3.8 | 3.9 | 3.9 | 4.0 |
| Radio, television, etc | 6.2 | 7.3 | 8.0 | 8.7 | 9.1 | 9.5 |
| Non-durables |  |  |  |  |  |  |
| Food | 23.2 | 24.1 | 24.6 | 25.0 | 25.4 | 25.6 |
| Beers | 4.9 | 4.9 | 5.1 | 5.2 | 5.2 | 5.2 |
| Wines and spirits | 5.3 | 5.3 | 5.9 | 6.4 | 7.2 | 7.8 |
| Tobacco | 3.8 | 3.7 | 3.6 | 3.5 | 3.5 | 3.4 |
| Clothing | 10.3 | 11.1 | 12.0 | 12.9 | 13.5 | 14.2 |
| Footwear | 2.1 | 2.2 | 2.3 | 2.5 | 2.6 | 2.8 |
| Energy products | 11.8 | 12.3 | 12.6 | 13.0 | 13.2 | 13.4 |
| Other goods | 16.5 | 17.3 | 18.2 | 19.2 | 19.8 | 20.2 |
| Rent, rates, etc | 17.1 | 17.3 | 17.5 | 17.8 | 18.1 | 18.5 |
| Other services | 39.1 | 41.4 | 43.9 | 46.6 | 47.9 | 49.1 |
| Total | 152.0 | 159.2 | 167.2 | 174.9 | 179.7 | 184.4 |
| Durables | 17.9 | 19.6 | 21.3 | 22.7 | 23.3 | 24.2 |
| Non-durables | 134.1 | 139.6 | 145.9 | 152.2 | 156.4 | 160.2 |

Source: *Economic Trends, Retail Business* estimates.

There are many interesting facts to be extrapolated from consumer spending statistics: nine per cent of all households now own a home computer, and nearly 30 per cent a microwave. The UK has

111

one of the highest proportionate spends on alcoholic drink (nearly five per cent of all household expenditure) in the world. But it is the service sector comprising one quarter of total consumer spending which dominates this analysis.

Greater affluence and increased leisure time for the majority of consumers not only means more concentration will be needed on improving the service industries' provision but it underlines the importance for all retailers to identify the consumer as a person rather than as a statistic.

## Consumer-led strategies

The third great phase of retailing this century has begun. The manufacturer domination of the early years gave way to a more retailer-orientated approach. Now consumer-led strategies are the name of the game; as indeed they have been for long enough in the wider world of marketing. Customers will never have had it so good!

Value judgements need to be made. New methods must be perfected for the clustering of discrete groups of consumers into niches or segments which transcend the classic demographic boundaries.

Upon what criteria? Market segmentation, currently much in vogue within the Burton Group and other high-flying multiples, is actually not new having been the subject of a classic address to an American marketing conference by Wendell Smith as long ago as 1956. Wilkie defines it as: "a management strategy that adapts a firm's marketing mix to best fit the various consumer differences that exist in a given market".

How and why consumers differ from each other and where, if at all, they share a common predisposition to respond favourably to a specific retail marketing mix is the task on hand. Not an easy one given the unparalleled heterogeneity of today's consumer society. Better educated, less deferential, more assertively individualistic — these are just some of the characteristics that currently inspire many consumer groups, particularly those with geater discretionary spending power. The answer for many retailers has been to adopt "Lifestyle analysis".

Again this approach is not as new as many commentators seem to imagine. Lifestyle research into consumer behaviour began in America in the mid-1960s. Consumers were identified not just on demographic grounds but on the basis of their activities, interests and opinions. "Lifestyles capture many external influences — cultural, demographic, social and family influences — and represent opportunities for various situational influences to occur" (Professor Wilkie). Consumer behaviour is also prey to internal influences and this has given rise to a branch of research called "Psychographics" which examines consumers in the light of motivation and personality theory.

These niceties of terminology are too academic for the fast-moving, volatile business of retailing and, in any case, confusion between different branches of consumer research is not uncommon even in the most learned of circles. It is the advertising and market research agencies which have succeeded most in translating these theories into practice by classifying consumers into value groups. These groups — despite their elusive, flashy titles like "pontificators", "passive endurers" and "chameleons" — represent a distillation of various analytical approaches and do at least provide a form of typological shorthand for marketeers seeking to identify their key targets.

Retailers who strive to know who their customers are (as well as who they are not and who they could be) have not had their lives made any easier by the death of Mr and Mrs Average! Robert Tyrrell of the Henley Centre talks of the emergence of the "cellular household" in which the ownership of duplicate durables and new technological inventions, allows different members of the same household to do their own thing in their own time. There is a variety within uniformity today that sets the individual apart from the crowd and away from the Joneses! Despite the existence of modern cult symbols like the Walkman and the Filofax, these ubiquitous and seemingly identical possessions in fact permit the owner to edit his or her own private repertoire or agenda. Robert Tyrrell calls them the "new connoisseurs" who pride themselves on "savoir-faire". They'll be valuable customers when they feel their custom's valued!

# Developments in education and training

Montague Lewis

*Deputy Head, College for the Distributive Trades
(London Institute)*

*The closure of the DITB in 1982 was a severe blow
for the retail sector; since then, however, it has
pulled itself together in a number of ways.
Crucially, graduates no longer regard retailing as a
second class occupation — they are interested in it
as a career, not as a second choice. And it is evident
that the large retail companies which have good
profitability records are also those which invest in
human capital through good training and
education.*

The 1980s began with an acrimonious and partisan debate on the merits of statutory versus voluntary training for industry which was resolved by the Government abolishing most of the 24 Industrial Training Boards and replacing them with voluntary training arrangements. Our own Distributive Industries Training Board was closed in 1982 and the pattern of "levy and exemption" for training within those organisations which came within the "scope" of the DITB vanished into the mists of yet another tried and failed initiative.

The major argument put forward for its abolition came mainly from the "big guns" in retailing — the multiples in grocery and variety stores with substantial and increasing market share — who accused the Board of being a centralised bureaucracy which was divorced from the industry. The responsibility for its replacement with a voluntary arrangement was vested in the Retail Consortium through whose network of associations something like 90 per cent of the industry could be reached.

The Retail Consortium saw its role in the emerging voluntary structure as that of "a co-ordinating agency for the member-associations acting as the focus for consultation with the Government, the Manpower Services Commission and other bodies. In this role the Consortium will be the catalyst for training developments which are rooted in the industry's current and future needs. Moreover, by involving people with direct operational responsibility for training policies, the Consortium will ensure that the co-ordinating role will be undertaken without unnecessary bureaucracy. The formal responsibility for co-ordination will be devolved to a *National Retail Training Council* which will incorporate representation from all seven constituent associations, representatives drawn from the Trade Unions, and Further Education".[1]

The brief given to the National Retail Training Council was:
a)   To act as a forum for the exchange of information and advice on

training matters between representatives of employers, employees (Unions) and the Education sector.

b) To identify areas of training activity which in the view of the Council require examination.

c) To make recommendations, should these arise out of discussions, to the representatives' respective bodies for their consideration.[1]

The contrast between the statutory and the voluntary could not have been made more explicit — from now on training would be left largely to individual businesses to arrange voluntarily according to their own needs.

An early assessment of the new voluntary arrangements was made by the Distributive Trades EDC[2] when in a paper to the National Economic Development Council in November 1983 the then Chairman of the Manpower Services Commission identified distribution as an area where "training appeared to warrant priority attention". For voluntary training to be successful it was presupposed that businesses had the resources and expertise accurately to analyse their systems, the tasks to be performed in operating them and the skill and development needs of individual employees. The EDC Working Group recognised that many businesses were so equipped but considered that many others — particularly among the small and medium-sized businesses needed external guidance and additional facilities, e.g. in 1982, 36 per cent of employment in retailing was in single shop businesses.

There was an implicit assumption within the voluntary scheme that these needs could be met by trade associations, colleges, and trade-affiliated associations as providers of training and educational courses, training manuals, films, and similar training material. However, the EDC group recognised that the training services of some of the specialist retailing trade associations had been reduced as a result of the loss of the financial and technical services formerly available from the DITB.

It was recognised that the National Retail Training Council's role was still at the formative stage and that it was not yet clear whether it should undertake some form of monitoring of training among retailers or provide some other reference point for training in the trade.

Help for the NRTC was luckily on the way since from its inception it had lacked any financial underpinning to support even its own modest voluntary arrangements and suggestions with a modicum of clerical or administrative help. With the winding-up of the DITB there appeared a sum of £4m of residual assets and with it another furious debate as to the best use of these funds in the interests of distribution training, with many associations and individual organisations bidding for control of the funds. This was resolved by forming the Distributive Industries Training Trust (DITT) on 1 May, 1984.

The DITT fund was set up by the Department of Employment, and trustees appointed with a brief from the MSC. The main intention of the Trust is to use the income from the £4m capital fund to support:

— A wide application of training in the Distributive Industries with some emphasis on innovative developments;
— Training and development for young people in the age group 17-27 will be particularly encouraged;
— Some priority for training in pump-priming projects.

## A ten-year life

Sixteen trustees were appointed; eight from the retail sector, four from the wholesale sector, two from the trade unions, and two from education. All were appointed as individuals and not as delegates or representatives. The original idea is for the fund to have a life of approximately ten years, and thus in the first years only the interest will be distributed, followed by the capital in later years.

There are two main sub-committees, one for wholesaling and one for retailing. The wholesaling sub-committee is responsible for allocating about 16 per cent of the income per annum, i.e. about £60K; the retailing sub-committee about 64 per cent, i.e. about £260K; and there is a General Fund supervised by the Managing Trustees as a whole to deal with special initiatives and is responsible for the balance of about 20 per cent, i.e. about £100K.

The basic policies of the trustees appear to be that the wholesaling sub-committee is keen to support initiatives which might not take place without pump-priming from an external source, where for instance costs could only be met by unacceptably high fees from trainees, or where the numbers in a particular area are so small that a course would be uneconomic. There is also a commitment to short courses which can be repeated as part of a national programme. The retailing sub-committee is particularly interested in the 17-27 age-group, training to cope with the new technology, and with post-induction supervisory and management training.

In keeping with the policy of voluntary arrangements the DITT works mainly through trade associations supporting the medium and smaller sized companies and assuming that the large organisations will have their own effective training arrangements. In terms of the size of the workforce in retailing and wholesaling — about three million — the Trust's funds are tiny, but within their own modest remit they have been able to give substantial help to a number of organisations since their inception, and especially to joint industry-education initiatives linked to a national network of induction and short-course provision.

The debate on the development of vocational training in the '80s began as a result of the publication of the "New Training Initiative" which was adopted by the Manpower Services Commission and accepted by the Government in 1981. The NTI was formulated at the beginning of the decade in a context of rising unemployment — then just over two million, and now over three million — due to the recession and the consequent restructuring of industry. This seminal policy document set three objectives for the radical redirection of training in the coming years:

— To improve effectiveness by ensuring relevance, training to objective standards, and improving flexibility of delivery;

— To move towards comprehensive vocational education, to standards, for young people entering the labour market;

— To open up access to training and retraining for adults, employed or unemployed, to enable them to acquire, increase or update their skills and knowledge.

In introducing the New Training Initiative, the then Secretary of State for Employment, Mr. James Prior (now Lord Prior), clearly stated that "training was an investment and therefore primarily a responsibility for industry. Training is simply not given sufficient priority in Britain", he continued. "Like other investments it requires sacrifices now in return for future gains, but the pay-off is rarely immediate and individuals' and companies' perspectives tend to be short . . . We have to break through this barrier".[3]

The barrier that Mr. Prior referred to was not only employers' attitudes to training as an investment but to the lack of "willingness to do more for people and a readiness to make the resources of the workplace available for learning and work experience, especially for young people".[3]

Mr. Prior's comments took place against a background in which skill shortages persisted in spite of high levels of unemployment; the continuing disappearance of limited-skill jobs — over 600,000 lost between 1971 and 1980 with many more in the ensuing years; the diminishing number of manufacturing and blue-collar jobs which were eventually outnumbered by white-collar and service jobs by the mid-'80s; that one in six of all those unemployed was under 19; and that only about half of the young people in Britain continued in full-time education or futher vocational training after reaching the minimum school leaving age.

Although several training initiatives were already under way and being strongly promoted by the Manpower Services commission, such as the Unified Vocational Preparation (UVP) scheme and the Youth Opportunities Programme (YOPs) it was becoming increasingly obvious that these programmes, though well-meaning, were insufficient to solve the crucial challenges of recession, unemployment, restructuring of industry, and of preparation for the future.

## The Youth Training Scheme

The major response came with the paper "Training for Jobs"[4] which the then chairman of the Manpower Services Commission, Mr. David Young (now Lord Young) presented in November 1983, which outlined proposals for future training in industry and commerce. Its most important recommendation was the establishment of the *Youth Training Scheme* as the main route to employment for young people, and the development of *market-led* skills training linked to the introduction of new technology.

The size and scope of the scheme was breath-taking with the MSC initial commitment in 1984 to look after about 350,000 YTS trainees, about 50 per cent of all 16-year-old school leavers, who were seeking work. Most of the trainees were placed in four key industries — distributive trades, construction, miscellaneous services and mechanical engineering — with the distributive trades accounting for about 18 per cent, nearly 70,000, of total YTS trainees.

The YTS scheme for the distributive trades took off rapidly with individual training schemes designed and established early in 1984 using employers and "managing agents", a new breed whose role was to run YTS on behalf of the MSC.

The aims of YTS were to equip young people to adapt to the demands of employment, to have a fuller appreciation of the world of industry and business, and to develop basic and recognised skills which employers would require. A key feature of the new scheme was linking and integrating the skills learned and acquired at the workplace with an off-the-job element of training or further education which would take into account both the demands of local labour markets and the individual needs of the trainees.

Thus the main elements of the new scheme included occupationally-based training provided within one of eleven Occupational Training Families (OTFs), a concept developed by the Institute of Manpower Studies for the MSC. An occupational training family is a group of occupations which appears to have a number of key skills and abilities in common, e.g. for distribution it was *Personal Service and Sales — Satisfying the needs of individual customers.*

By categorising these skills and abilities into a small number of groups it was hoped that the YTS would enable young people to make the transfer of training from one occupation to another, because they saw the skill relationship between different jobs, and also to maintain a flexible approach to training, so that employees should no longer accept that they were "trained for life" but would recognise that certain skills became obsolete over time and needed replacement with others.

The major changes in training programmes were parallelled by, and also led to, significant developments in the Further and Higher Education sectors. The debate on training had been part of a wider debate on education which began in the mid-'70s with the Prime Minister, James Callaghan's "Great Debate" and continues to this day without apparent resolution.

The further education sector suffered from two major threats in the beginning of the '80s, firstly the results of the recession and increasing unemployment meant that their traditional clients — apprentices and young people on day-release or block-release — were greatly diminished in numbers, which, added to the loss of Training Board grants and other support, meant a substantial weakening in the demand for their courses; and secondly a sustained campaign from industry and government suggested that the education sector was not "delivering the goods" in terms of relevance of courses for the needs of the country and the economy. Additionally there were organisational problems which resulted from the introduction of the new BEC and TEC courses with their programmes of integrated studies, which entailed substantial curriculum changes and development at a time when resources were in short supply.

The most important response to this challenge to distribution courses came with the development of the National Association of Colleges in Distributive Education and Training (NACDET) from 1983. A consortium of six colleges — Cassio, CDT, Monkwearmouth, Plymouth, Portsmouth, and Solihull — originally decided to co-operate in producing courses acceptable to the retail trade, mainly because it was known that the trade did not support the BEC (now BTEC) format as it involved too long a time scale to train potential junior managers for the retail trade.

After successfully launching the Foundation Certificate in Retail Management with strong support from the trade, the consortium gained further national support and subsumed the Distributive Trades Education and Training Council (DTETC) within its association, and now has a membership of over 40 Colleges and industrialists. NACDET has also assumed a national role in terms of co-ordinating Further Education's national response to the YTS schemes and of trying to ensure that there is a qualitative, but objective, standard for all suppliers of "off-the-job" training to adhere to.

## Training framework

The result of this approach has been their work with the Retail Consortium Training Working Group, the National Retail Training Council and the MSC Vocational Education and Training Group in developing a nationally recognised training framework for the retail shops sector of the distributive industry.[5] The need for a nationally recognised course becomes obvious when one looks at the current menu of courses available to the industry and delivered by colleges, as in Table 1.

It is no surprise that the MSC cut through this tangled path to produce their "Training Information Base"[5] to establish new vocational qualifications which meet the criteria for the retail and distributive industry as identified by the *Review of Vocational Qualifications Working Group (RVQ)*. This Working Group

**Table 1**

| | |
|---|---|
| Vocational Preparation | RSA |
| Pitman Level 1 | Pitman |
| Level 2 | Pitman |
| Level 3 | Pitman |
| CPVE | BTEC/City and Guilds |
| First Award | BTEC |
| Vocational Certificate | RSA |
| 9441, 9442, 727, 700 | City and Guilds |
| Product Module 1 | IGD |
| Module 2 | IGD |
| National Certificate | BTEC |
| Certificate | NEBSS |
| Diploma in Grocery Distribution | IGD |
| Membership | Institute of Meat |
| Higher National | BTEC |
| CMS | BTEC |
| FCRM | NACDET/BTEC |
| Open Learning | DIOL |

reported in April 1986[6] and recommended that all vocational qualifications should eventually fall into a national framework to be called the National Vocational Qualification (NVQ), that the framework should have four levels and that a National Council for Vocational Qualifications (NCVQ) should be set up to implement the changes. This council has now been established and is working to this brief.

As part of its research, the Review of Vocational Qualifications had analysed current provision in Retail Distribution and observed that:

"For the majority of employees and employers there is no clear, perceived link between skills and competences required in the industry, and vocational qualifications that are currently offered. There is also no clear link between jobs or career paths in a company or in the industry and the acquisition of formal vocational qualifications. Many employers prefer to identify the skills and competences they need and to provide their own training for these".[6]

The four-level structure as proposed by the NCVQ is:

(i) Occupational competence in performing a range of tasks under supervision.

(ii) Occupational competence in performing a wider, more demanding range of tasks with limited supervision.
(iii) Occupational competence required for satisfactory, responsible performance in a defined occupation or range of jobs.
(iv) Competence to design and specify defined tasks, products or processes and to accept responsibility for the work of others.

In a study undertaken by the Further Education Unit into Retailing and the NVQ[7] this suggested that the four levels could produce the following structure within the industry:

(i) Competent sales person.
(ii) First-level supervision or senior sales person.
(iii) First-level management, e.g. manager of small shop or a department in a larger store.
(iv) Second-level management, e.g. manager of medium-sized branch.

Above Level (iv) should reflect competence at professional level with mastery of a range of relevant knowledge and the ability to apply it, e.g. managers of large stores and senior head office personnel.

## Ladder of qualifications

What is currently in development is a clearly-recognised ladder of vocational qualifications which is recognised by employers as producing competences in their staff, by employees as offering progression in their career, and by validating bodies and colleges as being relevant and essential to the needs of the community.

The increasing importance accorded to Retailing in Higher Education was recognised by the appointment in 1983 of Professor John Dawson to the Fraser of Allander Chair of Distributive Studies, the *first* chair to be established in the UK in the field of Distributive Studies. Professor Dawson now heads the Institute of Retail Studies established by the University of Stirling to act as a focus for study of the retail industry.

Another first in the field of Higher Education for the retail industry appeared in 1984 with the Manchester Polytechnic BA in Retail Studies, followed a little later by the appointment of a second Professor in Retail Studies, this one the new ASDA/MFI chair in Retail Studies, based in Manchester Polytechnic.

The importance of graduates in distribution was recognised at a conference held jointly by the National Retail Training Council and the College for the Distributive Trades in 1984.[8] What was learned here was that historically graduates were becoming more and more important within distribution, and that they were interested now in retailing as their first choice and not because they had been unsuccessful in alternative career choices. This is one of the most important developments in the '80s — that retailing is no longer regarded as a second-class occupation, and that with the UK economy now strongly based on the service industries sectors, retailing and its links with the leisure industry is now a fashionable choice as a career. But it would also be true to say that in order to ensure that this "sea-change" in career attitudes is properly fostered, there would have to be a much greater commitment on the part of retailing management generally towards management training and education than has recently been shown.

The '80s have seen major changes in consumer demand, tastes, and attitudes and the successful retailers have had to take account of these changes very quickly and professionally in order to survive. The development of the multi-strategy approach in retail marketing in response to low overall economic growth and a better-educated and more discerning customer, is seen mainly in terms of more investment in property and design — rarely in terms of investment in the training and education of staff to cope effectively with the new challenges.

Yet there is clear evidence that those retailing organisations which develop among their employees the ability to learn, plus the habit of learning, plus an ability to behave in a self-reliant way, i.e. those organisations which "invest in human capital", are among the most successful in the economy by whichever ratio they are measured and irrespective of the ups-and-downs of the trade cycle, as recent research has shown.[9,10]

In one of its last reports in 1981, a year before it was wound up, the DITB listed its priority training needs for the industry as:
1) Computers and the effects of technological change.
2) Distribution-specific training.
3) Training needs as a result of new legislation, e.g. consumer law.
4) Small firms needs.
5) Management training and development.
6) Young people and new entrants to the industry.

How do those priorities compare with the latest research into the needs of the industry for 1990 as identified recently by the Institute

of Manpower Studies?[11] They identify sales staff as needing:
1) Social skills for effective communication with customers.
2) Product skills for counselling customers.
3) Keyboard and diagnostic skills in making use of point-of-sale terminals and the back-office computer.
4) Entrepreneurial skills to ensure the viability of the store as an independent profit centre.

They also suggest that lack of training in the past was regarded as one of the reasons for high staff turnover which in turn led to mistakes, frustration and low morale.

Perhaps it would not be too much to hope that over the next ten years there would be recognition by all the industry that business success depends on staff with the requisite skills acquired through relevant on-the-job and off-the-job training and education.

## References

1. Arrangements for a Voluntary Training Scheme in Retailing. The Retail Consortium. May 1982.
2. Employment Perspectives and the Distributive Trades. NEDC. March 1985.
3. *Training Times*. DITB, No. 66. July 1981.
4. Training for Jobs. MSC. January 1984.
5. The Training Information Base for the Retail Shops Sector — Agreed Training Provision. MSC VET Group. December 1986.
6. Review of Vocational Qualifications in England and Wales. A report by the Working Group. April 1986.
7. Retailing and NVQ — A study of the application of the 4-level structure to the retailing industry. FEU. January 1987.
8. Proceedings of Conference 'Graduates in Distribution'. NRTC/College for the Distributive Trades. March 1984.
9. M. Lewis. Training — an investment in human capital. *Retail & Distribution Management*. March/April 1986.
10. Small Firms Survey: Industrial Facts and Figures. MSC. 1986.
11. UK Occupation and Employment Trends to 1990. Institute of Manpower Studies. Butterworth. 1987.

# Mergers and Acquisitions

Roger Cox

*The inflation of the 1970s produced an illusion of growth, which led to the failure of many retail managements to restructure their companies. In some cases stronger companies stepped in and takeovers and mergers resulted. Acquisition can be a speedier path to growth than internal development; but there are pitfalls.*

*This chapter looks at some of the major retail acquisitions of recent years: Argyll and Safeway, Burton and Debenhams, the formation of Storehouse, the saga of Woolworth, and Next and Grattan.*

Of course, takeover and merger activity has not been confined to the retail industry in recent years. Most industries have been subject to major restructing of late as global competition stepped up against a background of relatively weak demand. However, British retailing is not open to direct competitive pressure from overseas and it has recently been blessed by the biggest consumer boom for 15 years. So, what is different?

The answer is very little, except the precise nature of the economic pressure on the industry. British retailing has been in slow decline for years; we just happen to be seeing a particularly noticeable correction. At some point in the cycle the market penalises those suppliers who have failed to match their product offer with consumer needs. A compounding error is to fail to see the consumer as a moving target.

In Britain there have been too many shops of the wrong size in the wrong places selling the wrong kinds of merchandise. As usual, poor management at the top of some — but by no means all — retail companies is most to blame. Mesmerised by the 1970s inflation which produced an illusion of growth, some managements, it is now clear, lacked the vision to restructure their businesses to meet the competitive challenges of the 1980s. Predators looking for under-utilised assets signalled by low p/e ratios have then swallowed them up, sometimes only keeping a well known high street name as an epitaph.

Retailers have traditionally been horizontal integrators and no more so than in the grocery sector where both Dee Corporation and Argyll have grown mightily through the mopping up of the last few national supermarket companies and a lengthy list of regionals. The same is true of the retail furniture trade, or at least of Harris Queensway whose most recent acquisition, Times Furnishing, has given the company one-eighth of the UK market. This is one kind of integration where there could, conceivably, be a referral to the

Monopolies and Mergers Commission but these references have been infrequent in the retail industry. Assuming that the merger makes sense in terms of geographical fit, and provided that the price paid for the acquisition allows reasonable payback and that any post-merger behavioural problems are solved there are clear scale and experiential economies in such mergers.

Edward Whitefield, Chairman and Chief Executive of Management Horizons demonstrated, in a paper given at the Institute of Grocery Distribution Convention of September 1986, some of these benefits:

"In the merged situation, net profits can be increased by reducing the actual merchandise costs, (the single largest cost of every retailer);" he went on to say, however, that "long term sustained profit growth has to come from organic performance".

It is rare for retailers to integrate backwards. Argyll divested itself of its drinks business acquired in 1983 when it took control of fellow grocer Safeway in 1987. (But manufacturers have quite often purchased chains of shops, sometimes with disastrous consequences.) This is not to say that retailers do not wield control over their suppliers as Marks & Spencer and the grocery retailers demonstrate. By the same token, true conglomeration is not popular with retailers who seem to believe in "sticking to the knitting".

Retail companies are occasionally found embedded in large groups as part of a vertical integration. Gallaher with its CTN chain and the two national bakery companies spring to mind here. Divestment of retail chains may occur if there is no "relatedness of management task" (Hanson Trust) or if they do not fit easily in with core businesses (Guinness). Or, of course, if they are unprofitable.

Retailers are still to be found who see their trade as unique in its products and skills. This is to forget the impact that mass merchandising and pull strategies have had on retailing over the past 25 years. The mixed retail concept has been skilfully manipulated by a few retailers, but main exponents Boots and W H Smith have recently been rumoured as takeover victims. Certainly the display of unrelated merchandise in very large retail units blurs the clear distinction between product ranges which is necessary in the retail communication process.

The term "retail conglomerate", however, has been applied to one or two groups in that they are made up of a collection of different trade chains. A very good example is Ward White which started out as a shoe manufacturer but decided to invest heavily in retailing. The group's retail interests range from toys to DIY and from shoes to car parts. It is a mixture which is doing well in profit terms. Combined English Stores (CES) and even Great Universal Stores (GUS) are two other retail businesses which could be categorised with Ward White. Both operate quite a wide range of specialist chains and, of course, GUS is well known for its mail order companies.

## Multi-strategy approach

GUS has found an unusual strategy for a retailer. Its direction is old and conservative but naturally desires to protect the company and its shareholders in this age of discontinuity. The group has split ownership of its Paige Womenswear chain with CES which now operates it. The Times Furnishing chain has been sold in entirety to Harris Queensway in return for a substantial cross holding of shares. Perhaps more of the same will be seen in the future.

The GUS demergers are, however, just a sideshow at present in the changes which are occuring in the retail industry. The tag "retail revolution" has been put on the efforts of Sir Ralph Halpern, Sir Terence Conran and George Davies. In keeping with the changed nature of retail markets the above-mentioned "new retailers" adopt what Wood Mackenzie calls a multi-strategy approach where a retailer operates from several different chains of shops each closely targeted to a specific market. Good examples include Next and the Burton Group. Both companies have been involved in takeover and turnaround strategies in the recent past. Next, for example, has chains selling mens and womenswear as well as furniture and flowers.

In an unusual move, Next recently took over Grattan the mail order company. This is a further channel through which the group can reach different market segments. Burton, after a disastrous move into such areas as cameras and office supplies during the 1970s is now firmly back with its distinctive competence, the retailing of mens and womenswear in its established chains of outlets and in Debenhams, the department store group acquired in 1985 which it is using as a channel for its various branded chains like Top Shop. Storehouse, a relatively new group, includes Habitat/Mothercare, the result of a previous merger, British Home Stores and Richards, the womenswear chain.

Both these acquired chains needed a re-launch because they were being left behind by more aggressive multiple retailers selling similar ranges with more flair and marketing skill. Run by Sir Terence Conran, the doyen of British retail design, Storehouse was a creative source of ideas for each chain. (Now, a small chain catering for the female teens market, has been abandoned by Storehouse since its inception which underlines the problem of moving into niche markets — a common strategy today — which may turn out not to be viable.) An interesting slant on Sir Terence's management style in the takeover process is illustrated by a *Financial Times* article on 26th November, 1985. When Mothercare was taken over in 1982, one senior executive of that company was quoted as saying that the change came about by "consultation rather than diktat".

After identifying the consumer tastes of the time Conran took over stores and groups which had one thing in common; they had all been relatively sound operations which had lost their way in the retail world of the 1980s. John Richards, senior retail sector analyst at Wood Mackenzie, and one of the most perceptive commentators says "Conran actually does very little with the store groups he acquires other than motivates the management and gives them the leadership they seem to seek".

Other takeovers have been somewhat defensive. The story of Woolworth is a case in point. The author remembers comparing a photograph of the Woolworth board in 1976 with a similar photograph in the report and account of 10 years earlier. Of the 15-20 directors in the photographs, only one name was common to both. This was indicative of the poorly managed Woolworth of the 60s and 70s. Not until its sale by its US parent in 1982 to a newly formed group called Paternoster has Woolworth had a real possibility of fighting back from its venerable corner in British retailing. Since 1982, it has made three major acquisitions: Comet, the discount electrical retailer, B & Q the very successful DIY chain of super-stores and recently the 300 branch discount chemist Superdrug. Previously, Woolworth had failed to secure the somewhat similar but smaller London-based Underwoods company.

Woolworth, apart from developing its existing 800 strong chain of shops wants to become a specialist retailer and the acquisition of Superdrug is a further strand in this strategy. With all its acquisitions, Woolworth has encouraged existing management to stay on and run and develop the chains. Geoff Mulcahy, chief executive of

Woolworth Holdings quoted in *Marketing* (23 April, 1987) said "we give clear objectives on what each company must achieve, and the divisional management teams run them accordingly. From our end it's a very hands-on operation".

The Woolworth revival strategy to date, while redolent of management competence has been criticised as not being about retailing in the sense that George Davies of Next sees the craft. It would be fair to say that the Woolworth strategy is to pick up well-run retail companies in the growth sectors while steadily running down parts of its core business.

W H Smith, after a few abortive efforts in developing its own chains of specialist retailer took the plunge and consolidated its premier position as a record and tape retailer with the acquisition of Our Price records in 1986. The company also acquired the two branch Paperchase chain in the same year.

Another example of the defensive takeover is perhaps the Asda acquisition of MFI, the out-of-town furniture retailer. Asda, as a grocery multiple with over 100 superstores, saw that the UK grocery market was liable to saturate by 1995. The risk-spreading deal was masterminded by Gerald Horner, the best known investment analyst of the retail sector, who works with Scrimgeour Vickers. Horner saw that both companies had close similarities in the way they do business:

1) Both have built their businesses in large edge of town sites.
2) Both have laid stress on providing customers with what they perceive as value — good quality at fair prices.
3) They are both exceptionally skilled at promotional advertising.
4) Each is acknowledged to have a very stong management team in a business which, by common consent, has not always attracted the brightest and best.

### Short term performance

Of course, such mergers need time to bed down, something which the stock market, obsessed with short term performance, is not in sympathy with. Echoing this sentiment, Lex of the *Financial Times* writing in July 1986 more than half a year after the merger, said "The strategic fit between grocery superstores and self-assembly furniture seems to have passed the market by". A year later the group needed more capital spending on new grocery superstores and on the refurbishment of existing stores in order to compete in the market place. Clearly, operating problems continuously impinge on any grand strategy. The consumer remains a moving target and to ignore the responses of competitors can be fatal.

Moving on to the alternative strategic direction in which retail companies have developed, we need to look at the methods by which these strategies can and have been developed. These methods can be divided into three "pure" types:

a)  Organic or internal development
b)  Acquisition
c)  Joint development

We are not concerned in this essay with organic or internally generated growth which cannot, by definition, be pursued in a saturated market except by taking share away from weaker players in the market place. In the grocery sector the major players, Sainsbury and Tesco, have been doing just this. The dominant leading-brand groups in each retail trade are finding mileage out of their market penetration strategies, but the gains are finite and time limited. However, they are much cheaper, particularly in terms of management resource.

Turning now to failure, we can say that no UK retail combination of note has yet been de-merged on the lines of a Dunlop-Pirelli. (This is not to say that it will never happen.) Neither, as we are on the subject of failure, are there many examples of contested mergers in retail in the sense that there have rarely, if ever, been situations where there were two suitors after the same retail company. Targets from Debenhams in the early 1970s to Woolworth in 1986 have had to rely on their own and their advisors' strength and not on attracting "white knights".

Joint development or venture is often set up by two partners when the costs of development need to be shared. Sainsbury's well established joint venture with British Home Stores trades under the name of Savacentre and currently operates six stores. Sainsbury finds that it can gain merchandise knowledge, particularly in textiles very quickly and relatively cheaply. The venture contributes to both companies' profitability. Marks & Spencer and Tesco have signed a joint venture agreement to develop alongside each other in new out-of-town or edge-of-town shopping centres. The power of a joint application from two of Britain's premier retailers has helped the venture so far to assemble more than half-a-dozen viable sites. As other essays in this collection suggest out-of town retailing is a major option for today's retailers if only because the likes of Marks & Spencer need more space to enlarge product range and consumer choice.

On the topical subject of mangement buy-outs, while these have been popular in industry generally, suprisingly, they have not caught on in retail. When they have, they have tended to be unsuccessful. For example, the independent Wades furniture chain was taken over by the Asda group prior to its acquisition of MFI. This did not work and the subsidiary was bought out by its management. Wades has now been acquired by Gillow (formerly Waring and Gillow) which is putting an aggressive new face to furniture retailing. A similar thing happened with Timpson Shoes. Its parent — United Drapery Stores (UDS) — was originally acquired by Hanson Trust and the management bought it out in 1983. From then until 1987 it struggled along with the rest of the British shoe industry until George Oliver, another well-known shoe retailer, bought it. The Timpson case is particularly sad because the company, with expert advice, seemed to be doing the right things. Unfortunately, the application of conventional market principles, when every other competitor is doing just the same, against the backdrop of weak demand is not necessarily a survival mechanism.

Hanson Trust as the leading UK conglomerate took over Imperial, whose core business is tobacco. Hanson Trust has also divested all its UDS acquisitions apart from Allders. Few large groups (for example, Philips) seem to warm to retail, maybe because the management skills are somewhat different from those involved in manufacturing. Hanson Trust put the Imperial subsidiary, carefully nurtured by Imperial as an important outlet for its main products, up for sale. The Finlay Retail management attempted a buy-out but the 250 branch chain went to Mr Arunbhai Patel.

What then, are the motivations behind retail mergers? They are no different in principle from any others and they can be encapsulated thus:
i) To reduce unit costs through economies of scale in buying, operational supervision for example and to exploit current strengths through synergy.
ii) To increase the group's market share and general exposure and so make it less likely to become a takeover target (this reason has now become less potent after multi-million pound takeovers have actually

occurred — but who wants a retailer, except another retailer?)
iii) To spread risk by buying into a growth sector (Asda-MFI).

Academic research tells us that mergers generally have no more than a 50-50 chance of bearing fruit. Of course, this ratio is skewed by unrelated diversifications such as those from which conglomerates are built. It is a cliché to say that the more unrelated a merger the less likely it is to succeed.

Mostly those retailer-retailer mergers which have gone ahead appear to have succeeded. The reasons for this must centre on the fact that retailers have more similarities to each other than they have to operators in other parts of the chain of production and distribution. In retailing the human resource has the greatest exposure to the customer, and so the proper use of people here must be based on remuneration, training and team-building. In terms of people use and technical skills application, there is a similarity in management task in retailing. Differences do occur in the product area, although mass merchandising has reduced these problems for many products. Again, although there may be differences in the processes of retailing, instore formats have mostly adopted some form or self-selection or self-service.

Mergers and acquisitions will continue in the retail industry over the next 5-10 years. By then the survivors will have provided an ongoing and adequate product offering. New technology will also improve administrative efficiency in the areas of planning, control and co-ordination. No moves of this kind can succeed properly without the full commitment of top management and their complete understanding of what is going on. A growing interest in corporate planning in the retail industry over the past 15 years has increased the possibilities of better central direction and resource allocation by retailers in the future. Acquisitions and merger activity will moderate in retail as the next long boom takes us into the 21st century.

*Footnote:* The City's fears about the Asda/MFI merger have been proved right and the group is to be demerged. At the time of writing poor results of Storehouse have also put in doubt the future of this loose agglomeration of retail chains. Next plc has taken over CES along with Dillons, the Midlands-based CTN group. These developments only go to illustrate further the flux in which British retailing finds itself today.

# About the Authors

**Dr John Beaumont** is Chief Executive of the Institute of Grocery Distribution. After reading Agricultural Economics at both Durham and Newcastle Universities, he joined MAFF as an economist in the Food Economics Unit. He joined the IGD as an economist in 1974, and has been Chief Executive since 1983. Amongst other bodies he is currently a member of the MAFF National Food Survey Committee, and the National Retail Training Council.

**Roger Cox** has 15 years' experience of retail marketing management with such companies as Sainsbury, John Menzies and Philips Electrical. He then spent some time as a retail sector investment analyst in the City and for the past ten years has been a freelance consultant and writer. Apart from being a contributor to RDM since its first issue, he has had four books published on the subject of retailing.

**Rodney Fitch** is Executive Chairman of Fitch & Co Design Consultants plc, one of Europe's largest design consultancies. He joined Terence Conran in 1963 and became managing director of Conran Design Group in 1968. Then, together with four colleagues, he founded Fitch & Company in 1972. Rodney Fitch is a Fellow, Vice-President and Honorary Treasurer of the Chartered Society of Designers. He recently served on the Design Working Party at the National Economic Development Office, reporting to the government on UK industrial performance.

**Eric W. Foster** founded Spectra in 1980 and is now Chairman of Spectra Management Support Ltd, the group company responsible for research, consultancy and information services. His career in retailing includes F. W. Woolworth and Bata Shoes. He has extensive experience in the computer industry, and for many years has been associated with banking, manufacturing and retail and distribution, both as a supplier and as an independent consultant.

From 1972-80 he was ICL's Worldwide Business Manager for application specific terminal systems, for financial, retail and factory data collection applications. He project managed the planning, development and launch of the 9500 Point-of-Sale and 9600 Factory Terminal Systems.

**Martin R. Houghton** is Director of Information and Consultancy Services with Spectra Management Support Ltd. He has an engineering and management background and has held senior positions with the Van Leer Group (industrial automation), Solartron (instrumentation), Kode International (computer peripherals), The Racal Group (communications, security and EFTPoS terminal systems), and Logica Financial Systems (bespoke software development). At Racal he was responsible for the marketing of EFT and credit authorisation terminals which has given him an interest in retail payment systems.

**Dr Gil Jones** is Founder and Chief executive of RMDP, best known for its annual EPoS Congress series (now EPoS/EFTPoS). He has acted as adviser to a number of government organisations, such as British Telecom and NEDO; and to retail companies such as Wallis, and Thorntons. His expertise lies in management information systems and the application of computers to retailing, and he has been widely published in the form of books and articles in this field. Gil Jones was formerly a lecturer at Durham University Business School and at Brunel University.

**Dr David A. Kirby** is a Senior Lecturer at St David's University College, University of Wales, Lampeter. He has researched, extensively, the problems of the small shop, both in Britain and abroad and has held visiting positions in Norway, Sweden, and Japan. Prior to moving to Wales he was a Post-Doctoral Research Fellow at the Manchester Business School. He acts as adviser and consultant to various commercial and government organisations and runs management training programmes specifically for the small retail business.

**Montague Lewis** is Deputy Head of the College for the Distributive Trades, one of the seven Founder Colleges of the London Institute. He took his B.A. in Economics and Philosophy at London University, and his M.A. in economics at Brunel University. His research dissertation analysed training as an investment in human capital and was based on the experience of Marks & Spencer, Sainsbury, and the John Lewis Partnership.

Monty Lewis gained management and marketing experience in the clothing and food distribution industries during a period of over 20 years, and he was also editor of *British Style,* the international textile and clothing trades quarterly publication.

**Penelope Ody** is a freelance journalist specialising in retailing and textile topics. She was born in London, educated at Bristol and Cambridge Universities and spent a brief time teaching before switching to a career in journalism. She has worked on a wide variety of business and scientific magazines including *Retail & Distribution Management* (1973-74), and *Drapers Record* (1977-83), where she was deputy editor. Penelope Ody is currently editor of *Retail Automation* and writes regularly for many retail business publications.

**Michael Poynor** is Principal Lecturer at the College for the Distributive Trades in charge of all HNC courses, special workshops for small retail businesses, and other courses. He is also Adjunct Professor at Syracuse University London Centre running courses in international fashion retailing. A substantial part of his business career was spent with C & A, which he joined in 1969 as a Junior Executive; moving through marketing and buying he finished his spell there in 1978 as Adviser. He is a member of the European Association of Business Managers, and Adviser/Moderator to, *inter alia,* Shenkar University (Tel Aviv), The Singapore Retail Training Council, and the NIECC College in Zambia.

**Dr David Rogers** is President of the American-based consultancy DSR Marketing Systems Inc, but is in fact British, educated at the Universities of Bristol, Wisconsin (USA), and Reading. He was formerly Head of Site Potential Statistics for J. Sainsbury, and worked for American retail and consulting firms before establishing DSR Marketing Systems. David Rogers is co-editor of *Store Location and Store Assessment Research,* published by John Wiley & Sons, and has contributed to the shop location seminars at Oxford's Templeton College.

**Tony Rudd** came to Britain in 1968 to enter journalism after a five-year teaching career in South Africa. For five years he edited the monthly journal *Storage Handling Distribution* for Turret Press, and then moved to IPC Business Press as Editor of *Materials Handling News.* Eight years ago he established his own press relations consultancy, Tony Rudd & Associates, undertaking a wide range of freelance projects in the physical distribution, materials handling and retailing fields.

**Russell Schiller** became interested in retail location in the 1960s while working as a Market Research Executive for the Thomson Organisation. He was involved with optimising Yellow Pages and newspaper circulation areas. He took a Ph.D. at the University of Reading under Professor Peter Hall for research on modelling marketing areas. Since 1971 he has been at Hillier Parker working first on shopping studies and more recently as head of the Research Department. At Hillier Parker he has developed a database of property rents and yields covering a wide range of shop property. He works closely with retailers, developers and funding institutions.

137

# The Changing Face of British Retailing

**Steve Worthington** is Lecturer in Retailing in the Department of Business and Management at the University of Stirling. A graduate of the University of Hull and with an M.B.A. from Manchester Business School, he previously lectured at Trent Polytechnic, Nottingham, before deciding to focus his research and consultancy interests into the retail industry. Working within the Institute for Retail Studies at Stirling, he is course leader of the M.B.A. variant in Retail Management. Steve Worthington has shop floor experience with a number of major retailers, including Eaton's in Canada and the Co-operative Movement in the UK.

**James Woudhuysen** is Director of Information at Fitch. He read physics at Sussex University and then moved to the Science Policy Research Unit at Sussex. Between 1976 and 1982 he was Technology Editor and then Editor of *Design* magazine, and from 1982-86 he was co-ordinator of postgraduate studies at the Central School of Art & Design.

James Woudhuysen is Joint Editor of *Central to design, central to industry* (London, 1983), and *Robots* (Conran Foundation, 1984). He has written for the *Economist,* the *Financial Times* and *New Society,* and contributes regularly to *The Listener.*

---

**Edward McFadyen** has been Editor of *Retail & Distribution Management* since it was started in 1973. Before that he was Retail Trades Adviser at the British Institute of Management, and briefly, Director of the Centre for Physical Distribution Management (BIM). He has undertaken consultancy for organisations which include NEDO (EDC for the Distributive Trades), the Gottlieb Duttweiler Institute, and the DITB. He has been published in the *Financial Times,* the *Guardian,* and for a period was UK correspondent for *Libre Service Actualités.* He has also broadcast a number of talks and documentaries for BBC Radio 4.

He is a past prize winner of the John Player Management Journalist of the Year Award.

138